101

things your estate agent should tell you
when buying or selling a property

First published in the United Kingdom in 2011.

Edited by Jacqui Daley
Photography by Ben Millar-Cole
Design by Gemma Wilson

ISBN 9780956734105

A CIP catalogue for this book is available from
the British Library.

10 9 8 7 6 5 4 3 2 1

Printed and bound by CPI Group (UK) Ltd, Croydon, CR0 4YY.

101

things your estate agent should tell you

when buying or selling a property

David Pollock

Contents

Forewords

I love David Pollock. He is a great guy and a very talented businessman.

We've known each other for 12 years now, first coming into contact when he had his whole Greene & Co. team join me for a three-day training session on customer service back in the 90s.

David's determination and quest for perfection in motivating his colleagues and improving his business might appear to some obsessive, but his results speak for themselves.

David is, perhaps unusually, a very honest estate agent (!) and is definitely worth listening to.

So, enjoy the read. It's to the point, relevant and full of fantastic advice when looking to buy or sell a property (my personal favourite is Chapter 2 and the concept of the Balcony).

Julian Richer
Founder, Richer Sounds plc

When one meets someone and they tell you that they are a residential estate agent, often the reaction is one of caution, amusement and scepticism. It is one of these professions whereby often the concerns of the owner or those of the purchasers are of secondary importance, with the motto very much being 'let's do the deal no matter what'.

David, who I have known for many years, albeit very keen and extremely motivated, is one of those rare breeds in his profession that actually makes an effort to understand the needs and priorities of both the seller and the buyer. He is no pushover but he listens and considers the opinions of others and has made Greene & Co one of the niche and most successful agencies in North London.

What I find refreshing is his relationship with the members of his staff, where although the focus on achievement is very much at the fore, there seems to be an aura of appreciation close to reverence for David, in my mind because of what I perceive as his consideration and motivation he gives to each and every member.

Having read the book, I find the anecdotes amusing and very much in keeping of David's colourful character, in what makes him one of the most charming and unique individuals of this fascinating industry.

Harry Handelsman
Leading Developer and Chairman of
Manhattan Loft Corporation

I first met David when we were both starting out, around 30 years ago. He was a rookie estate agent and I was a young, nutty investor, trying to get started in the world of property. David ended up selling me quite a few properties and I must say, even from early on, I liked his style and approach. So much so, in fact, that when the opportunity arose in the early noughties for me to become a partner in David's property ventures, I was all for it.

Whilst my focus has been on establishing *Manhattan Loft Corporation*, with Harry Handlesman and *Yoo* with Philippe Starck, I've always had a keen interest in what David's been up to.

From an industry perspective, a big majority of the property world is about branding, marketing and understanding what the client wants. And David just gets it.

David succeeds because he looks at everyone's position in the deal, and finds the best outcome for all. That's why all the parties involved will keep coming back to him.

Soak up the exceptional content in this, David's first book. The man is really worth listening to.

John Hitchcox
Chairman, Yoo

When I first asked David in 2003, if he'd be interested in the BBC filming a six-part documentary about his group of estate agency's, I don't think he had much of an idea about the amount of time it would absorb. But day after day, for six whole months, our camera's were invited into the world of Greene & Co. You would have thought that being an estate agency there'd be a load of secrets, that we'd have been shooed out of meetings and kept away from perhaps, shady deals. But this was not the case with David. He is a man of honesty and integrity. And his company has changed my outlook on estate agents.

David has a lot of credibility within the property industry and I'd give some serious thought to what he has to say throughout this book. He looks at things through the eyes of the client, and what will maximise value for them.

He's certainly my first point of call when it comes to buying or selling property. And thanks to this book, he can now be yours as well.

Anthony Wonke
Director, The Property People, BBC2

Preface

I really hope you find this book to be full of tips and advice that assist you in buying or selling a property. My goal is to provide you with some tips, suggestions and thoughts on how to make the whole (sometimes stressful) experience, a little easier.

I started in this industry at 16 years of age, and over the past 34 years I'd like to think I've seen it all. I left school with no qualifications and walked the streets to find a job in estate agency.

My role models were my father, who loved selling (he loved me too), my uncle Cyril, who was a really successful property developer, and my uncle Reggie Shaw. He was the ultimate estate agent, running a huge practice called Druce and Company.

A few years later my father-in-law, David Michaels, taught me that a man could be successful in business and still hold onto moral values and ethics.

From there on I continued to learn from my business partners John Hitchcox and Harry Handlesman, from my friend Julian Richer, from all my staff at Greene & Co. and Urban Spaces, as well as from all the thousands of transactions I witnessed and was involved in.

But most of all, I learnt from my wife Sue, and my children Katie and Ben, just how lucky I am.

Today, and for the past 25 years, I have been the Managing Director of Greene & Co. and Urban Spaces. We've expanded to six London offices, and hope to open many more when the right opportunities present themselves.

Acknowledgements

The thought of writing a book was first suggested to me by Anthony Wonke, a very nice man at the BBC. They were three months into filming a six-part, fly-on-the-wall series on my company Greene & Co., entitled 'The Property People', which aired on BBC2 in early 2004. I think he foolishly thought I knew what I was talking about.

So, I started writing. Of course I got distracted, by life and business, and the first manuscript was kept locked away in a top draw for a good couple of years.

In 2007, Greene & Co. started to win a whole host of awards. We made the *Sunday Times Top 100 Small Companies to Work For* list in 2007 and 2008 and a total of 20 national awards over a three-year period, including *Best Estate Agency for Customer Service*; *Best Medium Sized London Agency*; *Best Medium Sized Agency – UK Wide*; *Marketing Team of the Year*; awards for our corporate and social responsibility; and even a *Best of the Best Award*!

Then in 2008, for some silly reason, I won the very first *Negotiator Magazine's Leader of the Year* award.

My marketing director, Jacqui Daley, told me to write a book outlining all of my experience – a quick, easy-to-read book for buyers, sellers and even estate agents. So, I flung her a copy of the draft manuscript. She took it away, put it into English, drove me mad with question after question and, well, here it is.

A special thanks to the following people for their assistance and their overwhelming support, patience and expertise: Simon Inglis, friend and writer; Bill McClintock, Board Chairman of The Property Ombudsman; Paul Marsh, former Law Society President and current member of The Law Society conveyancing panel; Simon Redler, Managing Director of Greene Financial Services; Nick Green, of Ingram

Winter Green Solicitors; Andrew Lester, of AML Surveys and Valuation Ltd, Tim Muir, Product Delivery Manager at Rightmove.co.uk, David Sandeman, Managing Director of EIG, The Property Auction Specialists; and Ben Gutierrez, Managing Director at Photoplan.

Note to the reader

So this is it…pretty much everything I know about buying and selling property. Some chapters within the book will be very detailed and pages in length. Others will have four lines and, yet, what I call a 'really good nugget' of information.

I have kept the book repetitive deliberately, to illustrate certain points that, in my view, shouldn't be overlooked.

At times throughout the book, you may question the order of the chapters, or perhaps the informal tone of my writing…but there is no exact sequence to buying and selling property. Each experience is different. I want to get straight to the point, skip all the fluffy, time-consuming niceties and help you buy or sell that dream home.

I've also tried to keep some consistency, using the average price of a two-bedroom flat in London of £400,000 for most of my examples. All examples were correct at the time of publication.

Finally, whilst you're reading this book, and during the actual buying or selling process, refer back to the points I make. Use the questions or examples illustrated to help get your point across. In fact, whether it's the advice I give or the advice of your professional advisors, use any, or all, of it to your advantage. However keep in mind, your due-diligence is crucial. Only you can be held responsible for the actions you take, or the decisions you make.

I hope this book helps.

David Pollock

1

No-one likes us... so why are we here?

Estate agents are amongst the least popular people on the planet, alongside parking wardens, tabloid journalists, and politicians. A Google search using keywords 'hate' + 'estate agents' produces nearly 1,500,000 pages. A similar search including '*love*' + 'estate agents'...well, it's not such an impressive result.

Let's have a quick chuckle at the stereotypical image of an estate agent; flashy car, tacky suit, way too much hair gel and a pushy, aggressive manner. We've all met one (or two) in our time.

However, I've got a little secret to share...estate agents are human beings, too. Yes, it's true. We hurt and we bleed. The vast majority of us are honest, hardworking, committed and give our best to people who are polite and friendly.

Don't let me confuse you, though, thinking estate agents should be sweet. Or soft. Be aware of where your interests lie, and think more of your estate agent like a football manager. You don't want the team manager to be a nice guy. You want him to be a winner. You want him to be tough, dedicated and not to stand for any nonsense. You want him to buy the competitor's star striker for a snip, yet sell your duff defender for a tidy profit.

So, if you're buying or selling a property and still think estate agents are the lowest of the low, go out, do it yourself, and best of luck to you. Perhaps you might benefit from a quick read of Chapter 6 *Doing It Yourself* before you go. If, on the other hand, a few tips from an experienced estate agent would be of benefit, please read on...

This guide is not designed to improve the public perception of estate agents. Nor is it about how to get a mortgage or repair a roof – there are plenty of self-help manuals on the market to assist you with just that (check the recommended reading list at the back for the titles we rate the highest). Instead, this book is a guide to the innermost thoughts and secrets of your typical high street estate agent, which I am and have been for the past 34 years.

Its aim: to help you get the best out of us.

2

Would you step out onto the balcony for a moment...

It never ceases to amaze me how often people waste money, making hurried decisions relating to the purchase or sale of a property. If I said to you, 'Here's a quick way to make £10,000' I assume I'd have your attention. If I then added, 'That's £10,000 tax free, totally legal and, best of all, it'll only take a few hours to sort' you'd probably bite my hand off. Or think I was a conman.

That's not, surprisingly, how most people react. Buyers and sellers alike, jump straight into negotiation and lose all common sense, sometimes trust as well, simply because the numbers being talked about are so large. It happens time after time: perfectly sane individuals, who happily spend hours shopping around to save £50 on a washing machine, somehow abandoning all sense of perspective when it comes to the biggest single investment of their life.

This is why, over the years, I have learned to advise buyers and sellers to step back from the whole process, and imagine they are watching events unfold in front of them, as if they were a neutral observer. Based on a negotiation course I attended at Harvard University, Massachusetts (taken by one of the co-authors of the best book on negotiation I've ever read, called *Getting to Yes: Negotiating Agreement Without Giving In*), I call this self-imposed state of detachment:

Stepping Out Onto The Balcony.

From this imagined balcony you can look down on the action taking place below; action in which you will often be one of the players. Think of it as watching a play, from a private box at the theatre.

Dr Michael Hall, American Psychologist and expert in Neurosemantics, describes the balcony perspective as taking yourself out of the 'performance', in your mind, if only for a moment. 'The only way you can gain both a clearer view of reality and some perspective on the bigger picture is by distancing yourself from the fray. Otherwise you are likely to misperceive the situation and make the wrong diagnosis, leading you to misguided decisions.'

Throughout the buying and selling process, whenever it's time to step out onto that balcony, the text will appear in a box, like this.

I cannot stress enough how vital it is to be able to look at yourself from this balcony and assess your own behaviour, as if you were completely detached.

Commercial decisions should never be influenced by your emotions. Learn to step out onto the balcony. Later on, I'll show you what we in our office call 'The Balcony Form'. Whether you're buying or selling, or both, the form will help you keep tabs on how the negotiations are proceeding.

By the way, how did you react to the thought of that extra £10,000?

3 **Preparation, preparation, preparation**

Yes I know you're busy. But believe me, clients who are properly prepared save time and money in the long run. They can also save a good deal of heartbreak. So prepare...for the best, the worst, and the merely routine.

How can I prepare?

If you are a buyer, see Chapter 21
      (Buyers: Preparation, preparation, preparation).
If you are a seller, see Chapter 66
      (Sellers: Preparation, preparation, preparation).

So if I'm a buyer, should I only read the advice on buying?

And if I'm a seller, should I only read the advice on selling?

No, read it all. Understand where *both* parties are coming from, and why they might be behaving as they are during an important stage of the process.

Later chapters specifically outline how a buyer or seller should prepare for the best possible outcome; however, the point I must get across to you now is why preparation is so important.

At one stage or another you are going to be entering into a negotiation. This chain will begin when you find a house you like, or a buyer you want to sell to.

What if you're wrong? What if you have rushed into the first flat you have seen? What if you negotiate a quick deal only to find out your property was undervalued? What if there is a big dark cloud on the horizon that you haven't bothered to look into?

What I am trying to get across is this: don't be a kid in a sweet shop, rushing in and going for the first house or purchaser you come across, then regretting it later. Each step in the buying or selling process, from the beginning to the end, begins with you preparing for it.

'And I thought this was just a property transaction. Instead, you make it seem like a military operation, or a game of chess!' you say. Good. You're mentally preparing already.

4

What are estate agents for?

Anyone can buy or sell a property without an estate agent. You can advertise your property in the local newspaper or on the Internet, you can put a For Sale sign up and you can most certainly explain, in detail, the wonderful features of your open-plan kitchen.

So, given the rotten reputation we estate agents have, and how easy it appears to do-it-yourself, it's surprising people use us at all! But they do. In fact, 90 per cent of all property transactions in the UK are conducted with the assistance of an estate agent – therefore we must be doing something right!

Here's what a good estate agent should do for you

If you're a **buyer** (or '**purchaser**'), the agent should introduce you to as many suitable properties as possible matching your brief. This means:

- the *type* of property you are seeking (i.e. apartment/detached house, number of bedrooms, underground parking, etc.);
- within your *price range*;
- within your chosen *areas*.

If, after the usual initial flurry of hit and misses – an inevitable part of the process – you keep viewing properties that don't meet your requirements, either they're not focused on your needs, you didn't brief them properly, or you're being unrealistic in relation to market conditions.

If you're a **seller** (or '**vendor**'), the agent should do all they can to get the best possible price for your property. Remember, they're acting on *your* behalf. You're the boss, so keep a level head, and don't allow them to get forceful (if you've done your preparation that is, and know what you're talking about).

They should notify you of all viewings with 24 hours notice, where possible, and carry out any viewings or open home inspections on your behalf.

They should call you on a weekly basis, as a minimum, to update you with any buyer feedback, how enquiries are looking for the upcoming week, as well as any progress on the actual sale and how they feel it's going.

They should make sure the buyer is in a position to do the deal.

They should be in regular touch with all parties – buyers, surveyors, solicitors and mortgage lenders – to make the deal as smooth and as stress-free as possible. Keep in mind, though, that the agent is not a miracle worker, and nor are you their only client. If you are, how good can they be?

They should be on the lookout for anything untoward. A few horror stories from my own experiences include:

- Properties for sale billed as a family home – but actually in commercial use as a brothel.
- Sellers using two sets of solicitors and dealing with two separate buyers simultaneously.
- Buyers trying to 'chip', i.e. reduce, the price just before exchange in an attempt to corner the seller at their most vulnerable.

They should be wise to the likely pitfalls.

Finally, on the day of completion, they should be available to hand over the keys.

And that's about it. Everything else an estate agent might or might not do barely matters if they aren't able to satisfy the above requirements. So don't be seduced by ultra-modern offices or glossy brochures alone. Ancient as it may sound, estate agents sell houses by hitting the phones. Everything else is what I call 'bells and whistles'. In fact, most of it, especially the press adverts and virtual tours, exists only to impress the seller.

5

How do you know if they're the real deal?

Most estate agents are honest and try their best, but not all are perfect. Even as I write, another Office of Fair Trading (OFT) report has warned of shady practices amongst the more unscrupulous agents in the country. You don't need any formal qualifications to trade as an estate agent and you could essentially do the job with a mobile phone and a rough idea of how to spell the word 'house'.

In my view, this isn't good enough; estate agents should be licensed. It's the only way to ensure a high level of competency in the industry. Although, whilst we're not licensed, regulation of estate agents has much improved. Since October 2008, it has been compulsory for all residential estate agents to join one of two redress schemes, approved by the OFT. These are operated by The Property Ombudsman (TPO) and the Ombudsman Services: Property (OS:P).

These schemes offer free, independent and impartial counsel to members of the public if they are dissatisfied with the service provided by their estate agent. That is, providing the estate agent is *registered* with one of the compulsory schemes.

A quick check of all local agents in West Hampstead, NW6, London, for example, on both TPO and OS:P websites brought back results of only 17 registered member agencies out of 25. This means that 32 per cent of agents in this area are not adhering to the compulsory code, and, if you re buying or selling through one of these agencies, you will ve no form of redress for any bad service received. The erty Ombudsman, with over 13,365 members, works hard to monitor agents, but with 150 amendments to the register every week, you can see how a few cheeky agencies might slip through the net. If you use an estate agent that is not registered, there is nothing that either scheme can do to compensate any unfair treatment.

To check estate agents in your local area registered with one of the compulsory schemes, visit the TPO and OS:P websites and click the 'search for members' link.

- The Property Ombudsman
  www.tpos.co.uk
  (Check this website first, as a majority of estate agencies are registered with this scheme.)

- Ombudsman Services: Property
  www.os-property.org

There are also professional, non-compulsory bodies that agents may belong to. Two of the best are:

- The National Association of Estate Agents (NAEA)
  www.naea.co.uk

- The Royal Institution of Chartered Surveyors (RICS)
  www.rics.org

Estate agents who are members of professional bodies have to adhere to strict codes of conduct, and for the National Association of Estate Agents (NAEA), an entry qualification is required – suggesting you *should* be dealing with a more informed, aware and ethical agent. I belong to the NAEA. This professional body has around 10,000 agent members and I ensure my staff study and sit the required examinations in order to achieve this qualification also.

As a member of the NAEA, I must comply with a Code of Practice and Rules of Conduct. Not only must I do everything by the book, so must the negotiators working for me. If they don't behave, I could be struck off. Mind you, even if I were removed, that would not prevent me from trading. So be careful!

Certificates on the wall are no guarantee of quality. I know of several agents who don't belong to a professional organisation (other than the compulsory schemes), have never taken an exam in their life and are straight, honest, professional and very successful within the industry.

So, to be sure you're instructing an agent who is honest and competent, you're going to have to do some further research. Yes, choose an agent who is a member of the redress scheme and preferably a member of the NAEA or RICS, but also look into what previous customers have said, too!

In these technologically advanced times, you'll often find glowing testimonials on estate agents' websites from happy clients, praising the fantastic service received during the sale of their home. However, there are also many online review websites where estate agents have *no* control over what is published. Type 'estate agency review' into Google and you should find some popular sites to compare your local agents.

The Property Ombudsman website also shows independent survey results for specific agencies. This can be found on their site, when searching for estate agency members in a local area. I would like to point out that from my experience, in the majority of cases, only clients who have had an extremely positive or extremely negative experience will bother to post a review at all. Saying this, if you live in an area like West Hampstead, and need to cut down on the list of agents you contact from 25, reading up on other people's experiences might be a quick way to eliminate one or two agents from your list.

No matter how much research you can do as a buyer, remember, the agent you deal with is working on the seller's behalf, not yours. He cannot lie to you, and whilst the OFT stipulates that an agent must not withhold any *material* information concerning the property, he doesn't have to disclose every little detail. These specifics are for you and your professional advisors to discover.

6

Doing it yourself

Despite everything I've said so far, I would still maintain that there is nothing to stop you buying or selling property without the use of an agent. This doesn't mean you should stop reading this book.

If you intend to buy without using an agent, see Chapter 61.

If you prefer to sell without an agent, then please read this book as closely as possible to help protect yourself from some of the pitfalls. Also see Chapter 100.

Here are just some of the factors you will need to consider:

- You will have to be sure of your asking price.
- You will need to spend wisely on advertisements.
- You will have to allow a lot of time for organising viewings and showing people around.
- You will have to be responsible for security. This means checking the details of buyers to ensure they're not would-be burglars. Always double check the phone number given by applicants. If you are in any way vulnerable (an elderly woman, for example), you must arrange to have another person in the house during viewings.
- You must be confident in your negotiating skills.
- You will need a good solicitor who will be ready to hold your hand when needed, and guide you when you haven't enough experience to know you are wrong.

- If money is a factor – and it usually is – the cost, time and effort of all the above should be weighed up against the likely commission charged by an agent (see Chapter 72).

Of course, you can always place your property on the market with an estate agent and still try to sell it privately at the same time (although don't try to do a private deal with a buyer who came via an agent, as this will make you liable to prosecution for fraud).

Would I do it myself? No way. Why would I want to sell my most prized possession without the help of a professional?

The Essential Nuggets...

Top Tips for Buyers and Sellers to Take Away from this Book

7

The Moving Flow Chart

Every property transaction is different. You can't say '*I've bought or sold a property before, therefore I know how it all works.*' It just doesn't work that way. Not once, in the thousands of property deals I've been involved in, has the sales process followed the same path as that of the sale before. With such a varied mix of desired outcomes, service providers, motivations, property types, etc., each deal takes on a life of its own.

You may have noticed the folded charts at the end of this book. They're there to help put some perspective on how things should (roughly) proceed. No matter what variables are influencing the deal, there are of course set tasks that must be carried out, in a fairly standard order.

These charts may help give you a flavour for when things should happen – and how long it may take for each component of the deal to progress.

8

The price rollercoaster

As we all know, property prices are like an economic rollercoaster and can seriously effect the value of your investment and future peace of mind. My golden rule when dealing with the price rollercoaster is this: it's not when you get *on* that should concern you, but more when you get *off*.

Don't try and play the market with your primary home. There are always massive contradictions, from a whole host of economists, lenders and experts, in the long-term view of the property market. So my advice is simple: if the experts can't agree 100 per cent on what's happening in the property market, don't try and outsmart them. If they don't know for sure, how are you meant to? Buy a home to live in.

Your home is your home, and as long as you can ride the market cycles, you're fine.

Compare this with the stock market: if you buy a share at 50 pence and a year later it's worth 30 pence, does it matter? The answer is no, unless you plan to sell it or are using it as security. Five years go by and the shares are now worth 75 pence. The fact that at one stage your share was worth 30 pence, and at another 50 pence, doesn't really matter because the only price that's relevant is the price you get when you sell it.

If you want to be a speculator, try a few hundred pounds on the stock market. It is more important to be able to sleep in a home you love.

9 It's the differential, stupid

On another money matter, it's not only getting on and off the price rollercoaster that's worth considering. In fact, if you're moving up the property ladder and looking for your dream home, it is important to remember that it's not how much you sell for, or even how much you buy for, but the differential that counts.

For instance, say your current home is worth £300,000 and you are planning on spending £400,000 on a new home. The differential is £100,000. Luckily, you managed to find a £400,000 property that, if you're quick, you can buy for £375,000. This means you can afford to let yours go for £275,000 for a fast sale, since the difference is still £100,000.

The outcome looks even better if you're moving up the ladder and dealing with percentage differentials.

Again, you're looking to buy with a budget of £400,000. You've found the perfect property and the vendors, due to personal circumstances and market conditions, are selling their home to you with a 10 per cent discount. This brings the price down to £360,000.

If you then drop the price of your property by 10 per cent, you could sell it quickly for £270,000. The differential between the two property prices is now £90,000, saving you the all-important £10,000.

It sounds obvious, but you would be surprised at how many stubborn people let a bargain like this slip through their fingers, simply because they're still holding out for the original asking price on their own property.

10

Speeding up the process

How much time does it take to buy and/or sell? To do it properly and get the results you want, typically up to six months is about right, as follows:

Step 1: To market and exchange yours (not complete): 8–12 weeks

Step 2: To look, saturate an area, offer and exchange: 8–12 weeks

Step 3: To complete: 4–8 weeks

All the same, you can speed up the process. Don't worry about nagging. Nag everyone; the agent, your solicitor, the sellers mother...don't take 'no' for an answer. Whether it's with regard to viewing a property in the first instance, making an offer, or getting a sale through. Nag your mortgage broker to ensure your mortgage offer in principle is through, even if it's before you've found somewhere to buy (you never know when the right thing will come up). Put on a thick outer skin and nag away!

We have a saying in the business: the longer the deal is in hand, the bigger the chance it has of falling through. Therefore, when looking to buy, minimise your risk by doing some of the following:

- Build rapport with as many local agents as possible. Deal with just one person in each office, know their name and call them every week. Make sure you're at the top of their list to call when a new instruction comes on the market.
- Don't be afraid to leaflet drop homes in roads you like. Talk to porters in block of flats which appeal and contact agents in neighbouring areas.
- Don't be afraid to speed up the process once you have agreed a sale. There are a number of tools you can use to do this. If you choose to have a private survey, find out which local surveyors are on your lenders' panel and instruct them. This means the surveyor who's carrying out the valuation for your mortgage approval will be the same person that's inspecting the property on your behalf.
- Get an email address for everyone involved in the sale, including that of the solicitors and mortgage broker. Then, on a regular basis, perhaps every other day, update all parties on the progress of the sale. If you're waiting for the surveyor to call you back with a time to inspect the property, copy that information in to everyone on the list; no one wants to look a plonker in front of the other parties. I know of one vendor who even created a dedicated web site for the transaction, providing each party with a password for access. Don't always expect solicitors to email you back, however, as this can be against the Law Society rules if they are acting for the other side.
- Always look out for things you can do to reduce delays. For example, if on the sale of a flat, you're waiting for some information from the managing agents, go to their office to collect it. Or call on a

neighbour in the block – perhaps they have the information. Has another flat in the same block sold recently? If so, maybe the same questions were asked and the answers could be somewhere handy. It might only take a few calls for you to clear a block in the flow of information.

- Watch everyone blame each other for yet another delay. See their delight as they pass the buck, and badmouth another party. Remember, insults help no-one, so what can you do to help solve the problem?
- Finally, not many people realise this, but if you're not happy with your solicitor, you can switch to another one halfway through a sale (your new solicitor will tell you what you need to do in terms of paperwork for this move). It's much better to upset an inefficient solicitor than to lose the property you're after.

11

Learn about £ per square foot

A more detailed method of establishing the value of a property, or to have a greater understanding of the market in general, is using the '£ per square foot' formula.

Don't be put off by the word *formula*. It's easy to work out, and is used often, determining investment values, refurbishment figures and land purchases.

First, work out the net square footage of the property. The agent should do this for you. Or, if you are prepared to do it yourself, here's how:

Step 1: Take the measurements of each room. For example, a 10ft x 10ft (3m x 3m) bedroom measures 100sq ft (9sq m).

Step 2: Add up all the room sizes; don't forget to allow for hallways and bathrooms.

Step 3: Now, take the net size of a property and divide it into the price.

So, a flat of 600sq ft (56sq m) valued at £400,000 works out at £667 per square foot. You can now use this value to compare other properties in the same area.

A better part of town will achieve a little higher '£ per square foot', but at least this will provide you with a good starting point.

It's not scientific, but it's a ball park figure and will certainly help – especially with the purchase of an open-plan warehouse or loft-style property.

12 Don't blabber

When buying or selling, never tell the agent you are willing to pay more, or will accept less, than what's currently offered.

In any negotiation you should never divulge your bottom line.

Say you're selling your property for £400,000 and you get an offer of £360,000. After a period of reflection on the balcony, you decide that you will accept anything over £375,000.

If you tell this to the agent or the buyer, I guarantee you won't end up selling for more than £375,000. However, if you keep your mouth shut, there is every likelihood they might increase their previous offer to above that of your lower limit.

The same applies if you are buying. Never divulge your secret upper limit. If you do, that is almost certainly what you'll end up paying.

Here's a line for you, whatever price you're offered or told is acceptable. Just say, 'Oh, they will have to do better than that,' then shh…and listen to their response.

13 The Balcony Form

If you take only one thing away from this book, make sure it's the Balcony Form (reproduced on pages i–iv). It is absolutely crucial to your success.

Think of the Balcony Form as a theatre programme, something you can refer to when you're up on the balcony, watching the production below. The Balcony Form allows you to consider the scenario in an entirely unemotional way. On the balcony you are a smart outsider, with no desire to see one side beat the other, but merely to see both sides agree and keep to the deal.

We need to detach ourselves from our emotional responses and only deal with facts. Sentiments such as, 'I've wanted to live in this street all my life', or, 'Is that all the cheapskates are offering to pay?' don't count.

The goal is to keep to the facts.

Complete as much of the Balcony Form as you can, as if you were the detached third party. Some questions might not be possible to answer, but the more you can complete, the better the overview gained. And the better the overview, the greater your chances of either completing the deal or deciding not to go through with it and moving on, without regret.

You may have to ask people a lot of questions and do a lot of digging to get all the information, but whether you are a buyer or a seller, try to complete both sections.

Under no circumstances fill in an answer simply because, as one of the involved parties, you would like to alter the reality of the situation.

Remember, the goal is to distance yourself from the situation and just deal with facts. So, if the answer to one of the questions is 'they're just trying it on' or 'they're just testing their luck' and that person is you, that's okay. Just be honest.

I often advise people to complete the Balcony Form before they make their offer. Understanding the other party's position helps considerably in your dealings with them.

14

The odds

Most buyers and sellers think that once a sale has been agreed, the house is sold. If only it were that simple!

Let's take 10 agreed sales.

Of these, on average three or four will fall through, of which maybe one or two will fail for genuine reasons. Most agents work on a 30–40 per cent failure rate.

Of the six or seven deals that go through, four or five will take far longer than both parties originally thought.

In other words, out of 10 agreed sales, only one or two will go through in the expected time span, problem-free. Therefore, you have a 70–90 per cent chance of delays or heartbreak when buying or selling a property.

Remember:

> '*I must not take this personally.*
> *I must not take this personally.*
> *I will stay calm!*'

15 Gazumping, gazundering and the Goodwill Charter

Gazumping

It's an odd word, 'gazump'. It's hated by almost everyone as a concept, yet depending on the state of the market, and according to one survey, it happens in roughly one in four property deals in London and the southeast.

The term appears to have come from the word 'gezumph' (meaning to swindle), and was first seen in print in 1928. In those days it referred to any type of swindle. Now it refers mainly to the property business.

Being gazumped means that, even though a vendor has accepted your offer, they change their mind and sell to another buyer who offers to pay a higher price. It's not a nice practice but, despite what people think, gazumping is not illegal.

You can minimise your chances of being gazumped by building a personal relationship with the owner and the agent and entering into a Goodwill Charter. Also, do not underestimate the value and importance of conditional contracts (see Chapter 97).

Many people are surprised to discover that it is the seller, not the estate agent, who decides to do the gazumping. Remember, the agent is legally obliged through the Estate Agents Act 1979, to put any offer they receive to the vendor in writing, no matter when in the process they receive it.

Let's say Fred Bloggs views a house where the owner is asking £400,000. Fred wants to think about it. A few days later, you also go to see the house. You like it, and quickly submit a bid of £390,000. The vendor accepts your offer and the deal is now in the solicitor's hands.

A week passes, and after careful consideration, Fred Bloggs calls the agent and offers the full asking price on the property. The agent (the same agent you're buying the property through) has to submit the offer to the vendor by law. What happens next? Does the vendor gazump you (i.e. pull out of the deal and sell it to Fred Bloggs), or do they say to you, 'match his offer, or I'll sell it to the highest bidder'? How high in the seller's list of priorities will be 'No, I've given my word'? (Incidentally, that's what he should be doing.)

The only time an agent will actively encourage gazumping is if he has no confidence in you as a buyer, or if you're buying the house via another agent (in other words, you're not his buyer and he will make no commission from the sale).

Gazumping leaves everybody with a nasty taste in their mouth, and personally I discourage it whenever possible. Too many times I have seen the second buyer (the gazumper), scare off the first buyer (who is being gazumped), and then change their mind on the purchase. They start to think perhaps they got carried away and shouldn't be paying that price; after all, the vendor was happy to sell it for less to the first buyer. Or maybe the second buyer suddenly decides it's not the right house and pulls out.

Where does that leave the vendor? Back at square one, or even further back than that really. By now they've also lost the original buyer, who doesn't want anything to do with the property, or the greedy vendor anymore.

In my opinion, the best position for the vendor to take should they receive a better offer, is to tell the original buyer that they have been offered more money. They should tell their buyer that they don't intend to take it, and that they won't be asking them to match the higher offer, provided that the exchange is completed by a certain date.

If this deadline is not met, then the vendor is free to move on to the second buyer.

By using this tactic, the vendor can keep the second buyer warm, whilst at the same time putting some pressure on the first buyer to complete the sale and get the money in the bank.

I should also add that I am yet to meet a single victim of gazumping who is not happier with what they subsequently bought. Gazumping can make a property seem tainted.

Gazundering

Another term that has cropped up in recent years is 'gazundering'. This is when, just before an exchange of contracts, a buyer suddenly lowers their offer price, in the hope that the seller will be forced to accept the reduced price.

This is another reason why sellers should never appear desperate, particularly when the market is flat or falling.

What can be done to prevent this? Not much, unfortunately, apart from making sure that there is a Goodwill Charter in place (you can read more about the Goodwill Charter on the following page).

Make sure you read the suggestions and the thoughts in the gazumping section, as much of it is applicable to being gazundered.

Why shouldn't you gazunder?

There is a big difference between a buyer seeking a price reduction due to a genuine reason such as a bad survey or a substantial service charge looming, and a buyer who is just trying it on.

If you think it's a way of saving a few thousand pounds at the last minute, do so at your own peril. I have seen cheeky purchasers lose all their costs as aggrieved vendors refuse to be blackmailed. I've also seen the vendors revenge, where they have been forced to accept a revised price, stripping the property of everything they're not meant to, and ordering superfluous deliveries to be made to the property, just after you move in (e.g. 10 tons of sand or manure).

Sitting on the balcony as the purchaser who has lowered the offer price, you can see the vendor is upset and agitated, his defence mechanisms have flared and, being weeks into the process, he is refusing to listen to any reduction whatsoever. Ask one question...financially, commercially, and ethically, is he right to react this way?

The Goodwill Charter

In addition to encouraging the use of the Balcony Form, I would also like to draw your attention to what we call the Goodwill Charter.

One of the most frustrating things for both vendors and purchasers is when an agreed sale, for one reason or another, does not go through. Unfortunately, in today's fluctuating property market, it is more and more common for purchasers to be gazumped and vendors gazundered.

In order to counteract this, we at Greene & Co. worked with our solicitors to come up with a legal document called the Goodwill Charter. It is designed to help stop vendors and purchasers from entering into sales and changing their minds halfway through. Locking in both the vendor and the purchaser with a 'goodwill deposit', it discourages vendors from looking for a higher offer once the sale has been agreed and those potential buyers from pulling out, or, making offers they haven't seriously thought through.

If either party withdraws from the sale without a genuine reason (the agreement can be made subject to the purchasers' mortgage offer, survey, etc.), their bond is given to the inconvenienced party. However, if both parties keep to the agreement the money will be returned immediately upon completion.

We think that this type of agreement will eventually become compulsory, as it seems to be the only way to prevent gazumping and gazundering.

Whilst I do accept that this charter may not be applicable to all sales and circumstances (okay, it's not the most water-tight contract ever written if you are in a chain, and heedless purchasers or vendors, even after handing over their deposit, can still get away with gazumping or gazundering), in the majority, it works. In fact, Greene & Co. has found that, by entering into this agreement, the risk of gazumping and gazundering is minimised by up to 75 per cent.

The agreement could be used as a method of testing a buyer or seller's commitment to the deal. If the other party is *not* willing to enter the agreement, why? My view is that anyone who agrees to the Goodwill Charter wants to play the game straight. If they don't, draw your own conclusions and proceed with caution.

A copy of the charter we use is shown on pages v–viii. Feel free to send it on to your agent and arrange for them, or your solicitor, to be the bond holders. Alternatively, your solicitors might prefer to draw up their own version.

Lock-out Agreements

Another similar concept to the Goodwill Charter is the Lock-out Agreement. This is an agreement whereby once an offer has been accepted, the seller agrees not to sell to any other buyer, provided that contracts are exchanged within an agreed timescale. In other words, you have an exclusive right to buy the house for a certain number of weeks. Theoretically, the vendor and/or agent should replace the 'For Sale' sign outside the property with one saying 'Under Offer'. You might want to check up on this. Also, if the vendor is selling through several agents, make sure that they are all aware of the Lock-out Agreement.

16 Dealing with the stress of it all...

There's no denying that buying or selling a property can be a stressful period. In fact, there are many articles out there suggesting that the home-buying process is the third most stressful experience in a person's life, behind divorce or a bereavement in the family.

I may have been around the game for a long time, but it doesn't have to be an ordeal. There are many ways to reduce any feelings of anxiety as you approach this very exciting new chapter of your life.

1. Don't take anything personally

You're dealing with money – and a lot of it. Buyers have a right to tell you that they don't think your bright pink water fountain is worth an additional £5,000. What's more, an estate agent has been involved in far too many negotiations to let you believe a vendor is going to accept your offer of £50,000 below the asking price. Regardless of what's said, listen, take it at face value and move on.

2. Know your stuff:

It's far less likely you'll be offended during the process if you know your stuff. Read books (like this one!), talk to local agents, research interest rates, and become friends with mortgage brokers. I'll say it time and time again: knowledge is power, and the more power you possess, the more in control you'll be.

3. Keep things in perspective:

At the end of the day, it's just a purchase…something you do almost every day of your life. Okay, buying a coffee doesn't quite have the same impact on your existence as the purchase of your dream home, but it's exactly the same principal. If this house (or the purchaser) doesn't work out, there are plenty of other options. There'll be another property listed in a few weeks time (most likely suiting your needs even more than the one you're freaking out about!); you'll find out a colleague at work has a cousin who wants to buy in your area; or, worse comes to worst, you can rent out the property whilst you wait for the perfect buyer who'll have their home sold within six months. Breathe. It's all going to be okay.

4. Return to the balcony

The balcony is your friend. It's your calm 'happy' place, where you're unemotional and rational. This is where you go to listen to other people's perspectives and, afterwards, make composed and balanced decisions.

5. Make the experience fun

Think about all the fun things involved in your upcoming move and the benefits of owning a new home, such as finally having some storage space, a room for guests and *gasp* a utility room! Every evening during the process, sit down with your partner and come up with something to look forward to once the sale completes.

6. Include the family

Once you're over the initial flurry of first viewings, why not take the kids along for a closer inspection of the final few properties you're choosing between. Let them see the path where they'll be able to ride their bike, or the road they'll walk to school. Arrange for only two viewings on the Saturday, and take a picnic and frisbee to break up the day. This way you'll get a feel for your new area and the kids will feel a little less daunted once the big move finally happens.

7. Zzz:

It may be easier said than done, but make sure you get plenty of sleep during the house-buying process. It is one of the best ways to combat stress.

Completion

Completion is the exciting day that contracts have finally exchanged and, all being well, the day that you can move into your new home.

Buyers and sellers

Avoid going on holiday in the lead-up to completion. If either side have any last-minute queries or complications, no-one will thank you for being hard to reach. It could also mean the deal might not go through on time.

Also, try not to pick a Friday for completion. If there are any complications, you won't be able to sort them out over the weekend. For instance, sometimes the bank or building society can be late transferring the money, which means it won't clear the vendor's account that day, thus rolling completion over to the next working day.

Buyers

Before completion, organise for your solicitor to have the funds from the lenders 'held to his order'. This means that on the day of completion the money is in the system early. Once the money clears the system (usually between 12–2pm), get hold of the keys and then change the locks. You don't know who has had access during the previous few months. Arrange for your local crime prevention officer to visit and install a security alarm.

Make sure you can gain access to your teabags…or something stronger. After all you have been through over the previous few months, you'll need a drink!

In fact, have a whole 'Moving-In' bag prepared. You're going to have boxes, furniture and paperwork everywhere, and will appreciate a survival kit to get you through the day.

In it, have:

Money for tips (e.g. for the removal man, pizza delivery)
Address book with all your required contacts
Mobile phone charger
Kettle
Tea bags
Long-life milk
Biscuits
Mugs
Small selection of cutlery
Toilet paper
Soap and hand towel
Light bulb
Batteries

Finally, all those grand plans you have to redecorate, modernise or alter your new home…if possible, try living in it for two to three months beforehand. It is amazing how many times you will change your mind about what you want to do. It is better to live in a bit of a mess for a while, rather than spend money on alterations that you are never really going to see the benefit of.

Buying

18

Are you absolutely sure you want to buy?

So you've gone to the trouble of buying – and reading – a book on the property purchasing process and you've finally got to the nitty gritty section on buying. Well, sorry to stop you in your tracks, but have you asked yourself this question: 'Are you absolutely sure you want to buy a property?' Perhaps you've been swept up in a tidal wave of advice from family, friends, workmates and financial advisers, imploring you to get on the property ladder *now* or forever be regarded as a failure. You must consider:

- Do you have an adequate deposit?
- How much can you afford to pay off your mortgage on a monthly basis?
- Do you have a fall-back plan for a worst-case scenario such as losing your job?
- What are your other financial commitments?

As an estate agent dealing in both sales and lettings, it's important to see both sides of the argument. By way of illustration, here's a rough calculation, outlining the difference over a three-year period between buying a flat for £400,000 with a £80,000 deposit, against renting the same flat for three years at £400 per week.

Purchase price	£400,000
Stamp duty and legal fees (stamp duty on a £400,000 property is 3%)	£14,000
Miscellaneous costs	£10,000
Total purchase costs	£424,000
Mortgage	£320,000
Mortgage interest for 3 years @ 6% on £320,000	£57,600
To rent the same flat at £400 pw for 3 years	£62,400

Now if the property's value rises, say at a modest 5 per cent per annum, this makes the flat worth £463,050 after three years.

Your mortgage repayments have been very similar to the rent you would have paid, except by owning it you would also have been liable for service charges, repairs, etc.

If you sell the flat for £463,050, pay 2 per cent + VAT legal and agent fees, it nets down, less the £424,000 it cost you, to give you a profit of roughly £28,000.

You might think that £28,000 after three years is a great profit. However, there are always risks, and property prices are not always rising (it's not easy to forget what happened during 2008–2009). The £28,000 could just as likely be £0 after three years, and a lot of hard work for nothing.

Renting is the better option if you are likely to stay in the flat for only one or two years, sell and not buy another property.

Furthermore, money is not everything (I bet you never thought you'd hear an estate agent saying that!). You're also better off renting if:

- You haven't the time to do all the research necessary for buying.
- Your future plans are uncertain (note that most rental agreements are for a minimum of six months).
- You want to get a feel for the area before taking the plunge.
- You haven't the time or inclination to sort out all the day-to-day hassles of property ownership.

A little story about renting before buying, to get a feel for the area...

I have friends who were relocated to Brighton for work. With only two weeks to research, contact local agents and arrange appointments to view, they managed to find what they thought was their dream home. A four-bedroom cottage, lots of light and character, a three-minute walk to the beach and a sound-proof, lower ground floor — perfect for their son to practise his drums. And, to top things off, the home was currently for sale and also for rent! So, with little negotiating, and whilst waiting for their London home to sell, they persuaded the vendors to rent the house to them for six months, with the intention of buying it after that period. What resulted, however, after renting for only one day, was that the two 'private parking' spaces promised with the property, essential in Brighton, were in fact shared with the difficult neighbours and, to top it off, squatters were living in a house three doors down and eliciting all kinds of illegal activities from the property. With a young family, this wasn't practical, or safe. With a few other small issues present, they decided not to buy the house when the lease expired.

So, whilst not always an option, renting before you buy, at least in the same neighbourhood, can teach you a lot about where you want to spend your future years.

If you still want to buy, after calculating the sums and considering the magnitude of the tasks ahead, read on.

19

Home sweet home?

Your house should always be viewed, first and foremost, as a home, a place to live, somewhere to create a happy life.

Never mortgage yourself up to the hilt just because you think it's an investment. It probably is. But life can change, values can dip, interest rates rise and circumstances alter. I've seen people, time and again, encouraged to buy a particular home due to its 'investment' potential, only for them to end up living somewhere they're not comfortable, or don't even like. The result is unhappiness, simply because they blindly followed the investment mantra.

If you plan to stay in the area for only a few years, or think you might have to move at short notice, consider the property's saleability. If it has been on the market for months before you buy it, why is this? Might it be equally hard to sell when the time comes for you to move on? In other words, would you be better off putting up with a place which is less than perfect, that may require a few renovations, but easier to sell in a short timescale if need be?

If you're planning to stay in a property for a while, how might the characteristics of a cheaper property impact on your future lifestyle? If it is too small for a family, for instance, how much will moving to a larger property cost in a few years time?

My golden rules to buyers are simple:

1. Stretch yourself (within reason) to as much as you can afford;

and either:

2. Take out a mortgage that's manageable to pay if it goes up by 20 per cent;

or

3. Only take out a mortgage of up to 75 per cent of the purchase price. *

(Options 2 and 3 aren't always possible combined. As long as you adhere to one of Rules 2 or 3...)

This gives you a little leeway on both sides. If you lose your job, you still have some equity in your home, and if the market drops a little, your investment will be safe.

Thinking longer term, in my experience, it is a fallacy that people are content to trade down when they retire. Sure, a couple will be glad to sell a £550,000 four-bedroom house, which is now too big for the two of them, but will most likely end up buying a two-bedroom luxury flat for the same price. A house is not always a pension plan.

20 Buying is instinctive

You cannot be sold to. You will know the right property for you. Learn to trust your instincts and the vibe you get; you might just feel the potential. Don't dismiss this.

A house which doesn't necessarily have all the features you want, might, in the long run, make a better home for you than one which meets all the criteria on your current checklist.

Don't be persuaded by what anyone else thinks. You're the one who has to live there. Don't be too influenced by friends and family. Their advice is always going to be too cautious, and their emotional response to a house will be different to your own.

Listen to your professional advisers but listen to yourself even more.

If you're not sure or have mixed emotions about a property, an increasing number of people find it pays to listen to (or learn about) the Feng Shui of a home. This ancient Chinese art specifies the placement of door openings, windows, furniture and so forth in order to ensure the maximum degree of harmony and happiness in the house. You can scoff at it, but there are elements that make sense. Having light-filled but draught-free rooms are bound to make a property feel more comfortable. If it's got poor Feng Shui – call it a bad vibe if you prefer – there might not be a lot you can do to change it.

And don't be surprised if the right property turns out to be the first one you saw. It happens more often than you would think.

21

Preparation, preparation, preparation

So you want to buy your dream home at the best possible price. If you do all of the following, then it might just be possible:

- Get your mortgage offer sorted before you start looking. It will save time and it's vital to know your financial limits before getting sidetracked by properties you can't afford.
- Work out your overall budget. This is not necessarily the same as your mortgage offer. Your overall budget should include all the extras: house-hunting costs, surveyors' fees, deposit, stamp duty, search fees, solicitors' fees, removal costs, insurance, redecoration and new furniture and fittings.

  Most people go way over budget when it comes to buying a new home. Will you be any different? Keep your feet on the ground and keep your head out of the clouds.
- Pound the pavements. It's better to walk than to drive when house hunting. Sniff the air, sense the light and shadows, and hear the sounds. Mark out the streets you like on a map. Mark out the ones you won't consider. If you have time, go back at different times of the day. A street that seems like a peaceful haven during the day can be transformed at night or over the weekend. Call into local shops and ask about the area. Sort out what you can afford and stick to it.

- Don't be pressured into a hurriedly arranged (and possibly expensive) mortgage deal, solely to secure a particular property, whether through an estate agent, bank or building society. Go direct to a building society by all means but do not sign up with anyone until you have seen an Independent Financial Advisor (IFA). The only products the 'Safe As Houses' Building Society will try to sell you are their own. That's why you need independent advice.

  You can search for local, regulated IFAs by visiting the Financial Services Authority website and looking on the FSA register.
  www.fsa.gov.uk/register/home.do
- Get your Balcony Form ready (see pages i–iv).
- Choose your surveyor and solicitor. Remember, it's not about the price they charge but how quickly they react to your requests and how approachable they are. Having professional, quality advice is invaluable in the house-buying process. More information on choosing the right solicitor and surveyor can be found in Chapters 51–55.

22

Why Mum and Dad should get involved

If your parents are in a position to help, try to get them involved. It's not just a one-way street; they can also benefit from helping you with your purchase. For instance, it could help them grow their savings.

To give an example: say you are considering buying a flat for £200,000. You're a first-time buyer and you're planning to live in the new property for two years. However, the flat is a bit small. Meanwhile, Mum and Dad have £50,000 saved up. In two years time their £50,000 would have earned them (let's say, and depending on when you're reading this book, 3.5 per cent, per annum) approximately £3,500.

If they put that sum into your home, it would allow you to consider a slightly bigger flat, for say £250,000. If the market rises by 5 per cent, per annum, and you sell in two years' time, you will end up with £275,625, or a profit of £25,625. Their share of this profit is 20 percent, or £5,125. So they will have done better than leaving their money in the bank. Of course, the market can go down as well as up.

Year 1: £250,000 x 5% = £262,500

Year 2: £262,500 x 5% = £275,625

Parents' return: 20% x £25,625 = £5,125

Another advantage is that you might be able to stretch to a larger property, of which a portion (either a spare room, en-suite bedroom, even a 'granny flat') could be rented out. This way you can use the rental income to cover the larger mortgage and, in the process, you and your family make a better investment. Buying a larger house might also suit if you plan to have a family of your own in time.

Alternatively, if you share a close relationship and if the house is slightly bigger, your parents could use part of it is as a base for visiting you, or making jaunts into the city. For a relatively small outlay they gain their own pied-à- terre where you live, at a far lower cost than if they bought somewhere separately.

Of course, you have to set this against the additional costs involved in running a larger home, including higher heating bills, lighting, maintenance, insurance and other responsibilities.

Another good reason to stay on the right side of your parents is that it can be pretty handy if you need a guarantor for your mortgage. Say you've just started a job and, although confident you can meet the mortgage payments, the building society won't grant the mortgage because you don't have enough of an employment record. In this situation, you can get a close relation to act as a guarantor, should you fall behind on your repayments.

Keep in mind, however, that your lender will require a guarantor to provide information about their own income and financial commitments. If they are heavily mortgaged themselves, the building society might not accept them as guarantors as they might not be able to meet your repayments as well as their own if you default.

23

Buying with a mate

Given the high cost of housing, sharing a property purchase can make sense for a lot of young people trying to get on the property ladder. Pooling your resources will allow you and your mates to borrow more money than you might otherwise get on your own.

Although lenders have become more amenable to this type of arrangement in recent years, some of them are still wary. So make sure you shop around, and don't take 'no' for an answer if this is the kind of deal you're after.

Another major reason to shop around is that different lenders will use different rules for assessing how much they'll lend. For instance, some will only lend three to four times the combined total of two salaries. Others might lend up to three times the highest salary, and one times the remaining salaries (up to the maximum of four).

Co-buyers don't have to have equal shares. The allocation in the total property value can be proportionate to the deposits paid, and the repayments you've agreed upon. This means that, if you and your friend were buying a property together for £400,000, you may put in cash savings of £80,000 and your friend may have no savings. In such a case, you would jointly require a mortgage of £320,000 (you can't have two separate mortgages) and you could still be 50 per cent owners, with you paying the mortgage payments on £120,000 and your friend paying the mortgage on £200,000. You would, however, both be responsible 'jointly and severally' for the whole mortgage. This means if one person defaults from the mortgage then it is up to the others to meet their payments for them.

Alternatively, using the same example, you could each pay 50 per cent of the £320,000 mortgage. This would mean that you would own £280,000 of the £400,000 property, representing 70 per cent ownership and your friend would own £120,000 of the £400,000 home, representing 30 per cent. For simplicity, however, it is easier if you have equal shares.

Before you take this step, think carefully about how it's going to work out in terms of compatible interests and lifestyles – not to mention attitudes towards cleanliness and housekeeping. If possible, spend a trial period in rented accommodation with your mates before buying together.

You will need to get a solicitor to draw up a 'Deed of Trust', setting out details of mortgage repayments and other responsibilities. You will also need to agree how and when the property (or a share of it) should be sold, so that if one person has a change of circumstances, or simply decides to move, the others must have the option of buying them out.

Finally, it is important that all those involved take out life insurance, and preferably critical illness insurance, too.

24 **Timing**

It is well known that the secret to good comedy is timing. If only the property world was quite so clear-cut.

Many people simply have no choice as to when they buy or sell; they may have to relocate for a job, they'd like to move during school holidays, or even exchange on a property sale *and* purchase within the same week. Despite the best of planning, schedules are easily scuppered when deals take longer than expected (which, as mentioned, is the case for around half of every ten transactions).

There are two ways of looking at the question of timing:

1. When is right for you in terms of convenience?

2. When is right in terms of the market?

If you have the flexibility, consider buying in the off-season. In the UK, these are the colder months of the year, from mid-November to mid-January, or, during the height of the holiday season in August. That way you'll have less competition and sellers may be more willing to negotiate. On the other hand, they might be more inclined to wait until the peak months to see if any better offers materialise.

Certainly the busiest times of the year for agents are spring and autumn. This is when potential sellers have had time to analyse their New Year's resolutions (or they've just returned from a nice break in sunny Spain) and finally put their home on the market. New, enthusiastic buyers generally enter the market around the same time.

Take into account the vital preparation period. If you intend to start physically looking at properties in March with a goal to be living in your dream home by May, you will have to start your preparations in January.

As to the state of the market, frankly, it is always a gamble. Even the experts get it wrong. You need to study what's happening with interest rates, what's being said in the press, and monitor coverage of house prices in general.

Have I mentioned before, look upon any future property as a 'home', not an investment?

Is it a buyers' or sellers' market?

A good indication of a buyers' market is when there are a lot of properties to choose from and little competition to buy them. Prices will be lower and sellers will be keen to negotiate. You should also see a lot more 'For Sale' boards and properties listed online.

A sellers' market is when there are few properties to choose between and a lot of buyers competing for the same homes. Sellers will not need to negotiate on their price and 'Sold' boards will be more prevalent.

If you're considering the market conditions, you need to ask yourself whether it's best to move quickly, or pay more in a few months. Of course, if you can wait for the right moment, it's better to buy when the market is either flat or just starting to pick up again. If you buy during the boom of a sellers' market you might well end up paying over the odds.

I will say again that, if you really are short of time and have to move, don't rush into a purchase. It's far better to rent somewhere for a while than to get saddled with a property you don't like, can't afford, or will end up struggling to sell.

Whatever the time of year, or the market conditions, it is always better to view properties on a week day. Your agent will be more relaxed and have more time for you. For most agents, the weekends are frantic.

25 Location, location, location

Okay, it's the biggest cliché in the property game and everyone goes on about it ad nauseam. Whilst in most cases it's absolutely true, location is crucial, the best piece of advice I can give you is this: don't become obsessed with it. If the property isn't right for you, however fabulous the location, you'll never be happy there.

Imagine yourself living in an amazingly located property, and then think about the mundane routine of your private life. Think shopping bags, cupboards, weekend guests, prams, cooking smells, toilets, cold nights, hot afternoons, sounds carrying, clothes drying...think car parking, schools, supermarkets, corner shops, takeaways, flight paths.

Don't be seduced by postcodes either. Try and dig out the realities of the area. Talk to the neighbours and local shopkeepers. Ask them about the things in the neighbourhood or the property they don't like. Then, balance that out by asking them about what they do like.

Crucially, make sure you do a trial run of the daily journey you'll have to make if you purchase the property, whether it's to the office, or to collect your children from school. Do the journey at least twice, both in the morning and evening rush hour.

Still convinced that location is all-important? Possibly not, given all of these factors.

Lots of buyers draw up long lists of specific requirements only to abandon them all in order to move into a particular postcode. Still, at least when they decide to move within a few months of arriving, the property is relatively easy to sell.

Incidentally, I was talking to the chairman of a huge property fund recently and he said 'location, location, location' is a fallacy. To get anywhere in the property game, it's 'due diligence, due diligence, due diligence'. Make sure you read Chapter 38 for more on this.

26 Getting in on the ground floor

No, this is not about obtaining a flat with a garden in a distinguished postcode. Rather, about considering the next *up-and-coming* area. Remember what I said earlier about your house being first and foremost a home you want to live in, rather than an investment? Well, if you manage to combine the following, you'll be climbing the property ladder faster than you know, as your home appreciates in value:

great house
+
up-and-coming area
+
ahead of the crowd

= a real winner

Keep your eyes and ears open. Study the Internet and the local and national press for news of new transport links which might affect a particular area. Public transport improvements, a motorway bypass or a new road extension can encourage more businesses and residents to move in to an area and dramatically improve the face of the neighbourhood. Look out for major private or public infrastructure investments that may have a similar effect, such as new shopping centres, leisure facilities, tourist attractions and sports amenities.

Also keep an eye out for any negative potential developments in an area, such as prisons or lap-dancing clubs.

Call the local council to confirm that there are no upcoming plans that could be considered detrimental to a neighbourhood. If you don't get anywhere during the phone call, search for public appeals currently lodged. It's a sure-fire way of informing you of what's on the horizon.

Search local authority websites for news of regeneration plans. Blighted areas often attract millions of pounds in regeneration money from public sector funding, the European Commission and National Lottery Good Causes. Key phrases to look out for include 'Local Development Framework', 'Local Plan', 'Renewal Strategy', 'Neighbourhood Action Plan' and 'Housing Improvement Zone'.

Check areas which are slightly run-down, but adjacent to popular postcodes. Look for positive features in the natural or urban environment which you feel are under-valued, and which may come into their own in the future.

You might have bars on your windows for a few years, but if you pick wisely, wine bars, coffee shops and quirky little boutiques will soon be sprouting on every corner, just as quickly as the demand and value of your property!

27 Buying at auction

It used to be that only property developers bought houses at auction. Nowadays, auctions are becoming more popular with the general public, with a substantial number of property exchanges carried out in this fashion.

There are advantages and disadvantages, and you must be fairly confident to take this route.

Advantages

Buying at auction puts you in control. You decide if and when you want to bid (and how much you're willing to pay), and if your bid is successful, it's a quick purchase, avoiding prolonged negotiations with the vendor. Since the sale is binding, there is no chance of being gazumped.

You can often find a bargain, although properties that go to auction often need a lot of work, so you must be willing to put in some hard graft (or pay someone else to).

Disadvantages

Before the auction you will need to have your mortgage in place, a survey completed, as well as the title deeds and all other legal documentation sorted. If your bid is not successful, you will have spent all that money and gone to a lot of effort for nothing.

Properties are often put out to auction because the vendor is having difficulties selling, or because they need major work.

Also, once the hammer has come down and the property is yours, you cannot change your mind.

Some tips on auctions

Attend a few auctions beforehand, so you're familiar with the process. Be careful that you don't get carried away and bid over your maximum limit. Make sure your survey is as thorough as possible. Most importantly, make sure that you have really assessed the property and decided that it is the home you want to buy.

On the day of the relevant sale, get to the auction early, and take a friend or partner along for support.

The Royal Institution of Chartered Surveyors has written a really helpful guide on buying and selling at auction. See their website for further information:

- www.rics./org/propertyauctions

Specific auction websites include:

- www.eigroup.co.uk
- www.propertyauctions.com
- www.ukauctionlist.com
- www.auctionpropertyforsale.co.uk
- www.eigroup.co.uk

Finally, there is no reason why you can't ask the auctioneer if the vendor will sell prior to the event. Often vendors will, if they think they'll get a better price.

28 Get ready to view

Some buying guides recommend making a huge checklist, with dozens and dozens of points to tick off before you will even consider viewing a house. This is daft. You'll drive yourself mad with questions like 'Is there a loft space?' or 'Can I eat in the kitchen?'

Say you can't eat in the kitchen, so you don't bother going to view a potential home. Sorry, but you may well have missed out on the most perfect property with spacious bedrooms and a beautiful garden (which were higher priorities), simply because you were fixated on 'the list'.

My preferred approach is to create a much shorter 'Must Have' and 'Would Like to Have' list.

On your 'Must Have' list there should be three items only, otherwise you're not going to focus on what is most important. Then, take some time to go and see all the properties in the area which meet those three basic 'Must Haves'. Here's a typical list:

Must Have:

1. Listed for sale under the 'absolute maximum' price you are prepared to pay – e.g. £460,000.
2. Located within your preferred area – e.g. within NW6, preferably on West Hampstead side of Kilburn High Road, but no further north than Cricklewood Lane.
3. Minimum number of bedrooms you require – e.g. looking for three bedrooms.

Would Like to Have:

4. Garden
5. Walking distance to station
6. Little refurbishment needed
7. Study

Putting any more than three items on your 'Must Have' list will make your life harder, not easier. And bear in mind, you may still need to compromise.

Buying a property that's an extra mile or two away from where you work, or has one reception room instead of two, are compromises worth making. Although selecting an *average* property just because you were bowled over by the view of the Thames from your bathroom is taking it too far. If the property itself does not work for you on a daily basis, then no type of view or quick walk to work will be a compromise worth making.

The cost of an extreme 'we have to do this to make the house work for the view' renovation, or having to move in a few years' time to something more suitable, often means that you could have stretched yourself to buy exactly the type of property you were after in the first place.

29 Doing the legwork

Narrow down your areas. You should start with one, maybe two areas as a maximum. Saturate each area and its estate agents. Then, when you have seen everything in your price range, widen it to another area. By focusing in this way, you might not find your perfect home immediately, but you will develop a better knowledge of local prices and the neighbourhood.

If you can't choose between three or four locations, no problem, just leave yourself enough time to investigate them thoroughly.

Walking the streets is easily the best way to get an idea of the area. You see much more than you would whilst driving. Plus, you get to talk to people and find out what they think of the locality. As I suggested earlier, ask shopkeepers about the area. Tell them what you're looking for, and why. They may well know of something on the market or, better still, something about to come on the market. And they will usually be honest regarding what's good and bad about the area.

Keep your eyes open for empty properties whilst you're walking around, then search on the Land Registry website to find out who owns the title (see Chapter 30).

You could also distribute cards or leaflets outlining the kind of property you like. You never know, it might prompt the owner to consider selling if they think they have an interested buyer.

If possible, make contact with the local crime prevention officer to check out security issues. If you have time, it's better to see them in person rather than talk on the phone.

Read the local newspaper and its website. Look out for blogs or twitter groups, to give you a better feeling for the neighbourhood. Once you've got all this information, compare it with the other areas you've been considering.

As you look around an area, take your camera, or at least a notebook, to jot down reminders. After you've looked at half-a-dozen properties the details inevitably blur.

Keep a checklist of each place you view, with digital camera images to supplement this list if possible.

Keep all these notes and images in a file. You may want to re-visit a house you've dismissed earlier. You'd be amazed at the number of times I've seen this happen. Also, the file forms a good basis for your hard-earned market research regarding prices, house sizes, locations, and so forth. You never know when this might come in handy.

30

Check the net

There's absolutely no substitute for poking around the inner recesses of a property you're interested in, or chatting to local residents about the quality of the neighbourhood. But you can also gain a huge amount of information through the Internet. Here are some of the more useful websites:

www.landreg.gov.uk

This is an official government website. You can download a title register for a £4.00 fee. It should show you who owns the property, the price paid, and any rights of way or restrictions on the land that may be noted on the register. You can also download a title plan for £4.00. For an additional £6.50 you can see the probability of flood for the specific property, but I'd take a look on the Environment Agency website first (see following pages) to get a general idea for the area.

www.upmystreet.com

One of the first online providers of local information, searchable by postcode. Free data includes local property prices, council tax rates, demographics of people currently living in the area as well as information on schools, transport links, and hospitals. The website also includes a local business directory.

www.met.police.uk/crimefigures

If you're looking to buy in London, you can visit the Met Police website for crime figures relating to specific postcodes.

www.environment-agency.gov.uk

Comprehensive government website with a clearly laid out section on 'What's In My Backyard?' covering issues such as whether your (prospective) house is on or near a floodplain, landfill site, or source of industrial pollution. You can also check the effect of local sewage treatment works, and whether or not nearby rivers or beaches meet water quality targets.

www.rightmove.co.uk

There are many websites simply rehashing the Land Registry Sold prices data, but not Rightmove. Their price comparison report provides an up-to-date indication of what properties are currently worth, sharing details and photos of properties 'currently' listed on Rightmove, those that are 'no longer on the market' including the date and last listing price when they were removed from the website, along with Land Registry statistics on the five most recently sold property prices within your postcode search. There are market trend reports and over 100,000 properties to search in London alone.

zoopla.co.uk

Review current home values; read property news; see sold house prices and learn more about a neighbourhood with the

AskMe!™ community message board. You can also view properties currently for sale and rent, as well as find the agents operating in your local area.

housepricecrash.co.uk

Provides house price statistics for the UK and Greater London; house price predictions; forums; and a really useful resource list with links to a variety of further property-related reading.

mouseprice.com

Again, listing sold property data, but also key local information; street rankings – listing the most expensive streets in a postcode, down to the least expensive; streets with the highest turnover of sales, and a heat map of the UK, breaking down average values and predicted growth over a one-, five- and ten-year period.

31

Book a day out to view

Yes, life is complicated and you're always busy, but you cannot expect to find your dream home without making some sacrifices. The best way to find what you want is to allocate a few full days for viewing.

Viewing properties in a piecemeal fashion just doesn't work. It's tiresome, laborious and makes it difficult to compare apples with apples. Weeks can pass by between viewings, and by the time you realise it was the first property you saw that best meets your needs, it's no longer available.

The best way to set up a viewing day is to contact *all* the local agents by phone and ask to speak to their best negotiator (it puts emphasis on them to be good). Ask them to register your details and send you information on all the suitable properties. Then, make a series of appointments to view, leaving a decent time frame between one appointment and the next.

If at all possible, allocate a weekday for the viewings. Agents can usually spare more time than at weekends, when they are often incredibly busy.

Set sensible limits. Any more than five or six properties in one day and the average house-hunter will be reeling with exhaustion and all the details will begin to merge into one another.

For security's sake, women should be accompanied by the agent, a friend or partner.

Don't take the kids, they'll just distract you. If you like something, you should certainly view it more than once.

This subsequent visit is the time for them to have their say about a prospective new family home.

You will save everybody – yourself, the seller and the agent – a lot of time if you're honest and tell them if you don't like somewhere within the first few minutes of seeing it. If your gut instinct is screaming 'no', tell them so and cut the visit short.

On the other hand, if you really do like somewhere, keep your mouth shut! Expressing mild approval is okay, but showing over-the-top enthusiasm will put you in a weaker position when it comes to negotiating. If the agent and vendor can see that you want it, they'll drive a hard bargain.

32 Make sure you're first in line

Whatever the state of the market, you want to ensure you're at the top of the agent's list of people to contact when something suitable comes up for sale. You want to be that lucky person, tipped off before the particulars are even typed up.

So how do you go about this?

First, as I said at the very beginning, estate agents are (contrary to rumour) only human, and have to put up with a lot of in-your-face antagonism from the public. Make friends with them. You don't have to invite them over for dinner but at the very least, remember their name. Keep their business card in your property file, and on it, write some personal facts about them, like if they're married or have kids. Establish a good rapport. They're more likely to find you what you want if they like you. A little charm never hurts.

Make their job easier. Don't just leave a home phone number with an answering machine. Make sure you're easy to contact by leaving your work, home and mobile numbers. Ensure they have an email address you access regularly, in case the agent sends new property alerts or important updates in this manner. Some agents even send brief details via SMS to your mobile if you're happy to receive this type of communication.

Respond quickly if an agent contacts you with a possible viewing. They'll take you more seriously if you show a willingness to view at short notice. Sometimes good properties go within hours. Be prepared to drop everything to go and see something if you like the sound of it.

Keep in regular contact. Whilst a good agent should notify you of the latest listings, it's easy to slip through the net when dealing with a large number of proactive buyers. Check their website, phone them, or drop in to their office regularly to keep your needs at the forefront of the agent's mind. Be flexible and open. Give the agent feedback. Help him or her refine their idea of what you're after, and notify them if your brief changes.

Finally, and most importantly, make sure you've followed my previous advice and have your finances sorted before you step through the agent's door.

If you can achieve the above, you will be considered a 'hot prospect', and there really is no better way to get an agent's attention.

33

What to look for when viewing (exterior)

So, you've pounded the neighbourhood pavements, you've done your round of first viewings, and you've narrowed it down to a select few, or perhaps '*the one*'. Now it's time to take a really good, hard, unemotional look at the property itself.

The first place to start is the exterior. These are the features you should be looking at:

- What kind of garden, balcony, yard or patio does the property have, and what state is it in? Are the plants and trees well cared for?
- In what condition are the fences, hedges or other boundaries with the neighbours?
- If there are trees in the garden, check they're not too close to the house (as this can cause problems with subsidence) and that they don't block the natural light to the house or garden.
- Check trees in the neighbour's garden, too. You don't want to buy somewhere with what seems like a sunny garden, only to discover that, during the summer months when all the leaves are out, it doesn't get any light.
- Is the garden overlooked by the neighbours? Has it got enough privacy for your needs?
- If the exterior is a mess, will it need money spent on it? Consider the cost of landscaping or other improvements.

- In what state are the outbuildings? If there are sheds and greenhouses, are they included in the price?
- If there is a garage, what state is it in?
- Are there any electricity pylons, mobile phone masts or other hazards nearby? Not only can they be potentially dangerous and look unsightly, they may also affect its re-sale potential.
- How does the roof and guttering look? Does the guttering look old, leaky or need repairing? Are there any missing tiles, or damaged chimneys?
- Check the state of the brickwork and the rendering. Make sure air bricks are well ventilated and not suffocated by overgrown plants or flower beds.
- Watch out for cracks in paths, external brickwork and uneven floor lines. All of these may indicate a problem with subsidence.
- Most importantly, go on your gut instinct.

Don't worry too much about checking every finite crack in the path or balcony. If this works out to be the property you buy, a surveyor will check and report back to you on any major issues.

Remember that any of the above negatives are no reason not to buy the property, just make sure they are reflected in the price. Ask yourself, 'If I could get £x amount off the price to do the required works, would I then want to view the interior?'

34

What to look for when viewing (interior)

You've got to the front door and nothing, so far, has prompted you to change your mind. So what do you look for inside?

There are so many factors and details to investigate when viewing an interior that I could write a whole book solely on this part of the process. But, as with every other step in the process, your instincts and experience will tell you fairly quickly whether or not this is the property for you. Just a few suggestions:

- What's the natural light in the home like? Often, viewings will be arranged during the day when there is good light (you'll probably find all the lights will be turned on as well, to create the best atmosphere). Visit at different times during the day and evening to check.
- Use your nose. Do any of the rooms have a musty smell? Look out for freshly painted patches, discoloured wallpaper or paintwork, or stains and 'tidemarks', particularly in the basement. Peeling wallpaper is another giveaway sign. Tap wallpapered walls or old plasterwork to see if they sound different in various places. A hollow sound can indicate a problem. If a damp-proof course has been installed, ask to see the guarantee.
- Check window frames and doorways. Cracks could be a sign of subsidence. Look closely for signs of rot or a patched-up job. Do the windows

and doors open easily? Is there condensation, often a problem in bathrooms with poor ventilation?

- Look for any slope in the floors and hallways. Anything other than a completely horizontal surface could indicate subsidence. Check the floorboards – if they feel springy underfoot, this could indicate dry rot (a fungus which may affect timbers, including floor joists, throughout the building). Feel the top of doors to see if they've been shaved down. This is another way to determine a subsidence problem.

- In the kitchen, opening drawers and cupboards will tell you a lot about the quality of the units. Similarly, what make are the electrical appliances (if they're to be included in the sale price), and are they still under guarantee?

- Check the boiler, fusebox and piping. How old is the central heating? Is it expensive to run? How old is the wiring? Are there enough sockets, and what condition are they in? Is there any lead piping in the house?

- Check your mobile phone reception within the home. Politely excuse yourself as you make a call to check the quality and range throughout the property. If you like the thought of being uncontactable whilst at home this may be perfect for you, but for those that work from home, a nightmare. Ask the vendors about their Internet connection. It may be less important to consider within London, but even some of the outer suburbs of the city have limited access to broadband.

Of course, these are only a small sample of the many factors you need to assess. But, remember, even if you do come across potential problems, don't let them put you off. You might be wrong, or the problems might be easily remedied. Your main aim overall should be to identify the most serious issues and have them checked by an expert before you make an offer, so that the cost of remedial and refurbishment work is reflected in your offer price.

Don't forget the rule, as applied to the exterior of the property, 'If I could get £x amount off the price, would I be happy doing the repairs and living here?'. Don't just listen to your gut instinct on this, obey it!

35

The infamous avocado bathroom suite

Though regarded as the ultimate in taste in the 1980s, the ubiquitous avocado bathroom suite can look pretty hideous to modern eyes. Indeed, a recent survey claimed that the presence of one in your property could knock up to £8,000 off the value.

My advice is, instead of being put off by the vendor's apparent lack of taste, you should use it to your advantage. Many buyers are deterred by a property's fittings and furnishings, but it is much better to see each house simply as a series of rooms, of particular dimensions, blind to their current décor.

This means looking beyond the surface, sometimes literally. For example, take a peek under the carpet, maybe there are old floorboards which could be polished up, or there might be Victorian floor tiles lurking underneath boring linoleum in the kitchen.

Keep your eyes open for hidden or unusual architectural features such as cornices and ceiling roses. A blocked-off fireplace restored to its original glory can transform a room's character and appeal.

Think of how you might also transform lighting levels within the property. Simply substituting curtains for blinds might allow far more light and air into a room which currently seems dark and gloomy.

Try to imagine what the place would look like once the vendor's over-stuffed furniture, flock wallpaper, garden gnomes and smelly pets have gone for good.

There is nothing wrong with saying to the vendor, 'I really like your home but I'd like to get a feel for what's possible. Do you have a close relationship with any of your neighbours who may have done renovations? I'd love to see what is possible.'

Follow the above advice, as many buyers simply don't have the imagination to do this. That avocado bathroom suite may, in the end, work to your advantage and get you a bargain.

36
Taking the long, green view

Energy efficiency is well worth consideration when it comes to your future property. Whilst it's increasingly important from an environmental perspective, not many estate agents will tell you that it will also affect your outgoings in the long term.

Nowadays, buildings account for almost half of the energy consumption and carbon emissions in the UK. The Government have introduced new regulations directed at raising energy standards in order to meet international commitments on carbon emissions and climate change. In October 2008, Energy Performance Certificates (EPCs) were introduced and have been required whenever a building is built, sold or rented out.

The certificate provides an 'A' to 'G' rating for the building, with 'A' being the most energy efficient and 'G' being the least. Ratings will be influenced by the size, age, layout and insulation, among other things. Running costs are estimated based on how the property will be used, the number

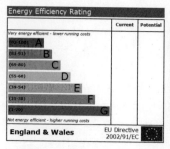 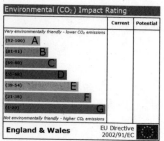

Sample Energy Performance Certificate

of occupants, etc. The average UK home has a 'D' rating. The EPC also comes with a recommendation report with suggestions on how to reduce energy use and carbon dioxide emissions.

It is important you take the time and look at the Energy Performance Certificate and understand what it says. The main area of concern should be the current efficiency of the property. If the property is classified towards 'G', then this will mean that the running costs for the property in terms of heating and electricity will be high. Perhaps the central heating system is old or there is little insulation. It is not unreasonable to highlight a poor rating or any potential expenses you may have to fork out to, say, replace the boiler, as part of your negotiation. Just keep in mind that the majority of properties in the UK will rate fairly similarly.

If the property has a poor classification, or if you wish to 'future proof' your new house for any other reason, you should consider some of the following:

- Does the property have double-glazed windows? On how many windows, and what condition are they in?
- If the house has cavity walls, are they insulated? If so, can you see the certificate?
- Does the house have a south-facing roof? It may be suitable for thermal solar panels to heat your hot water.
- Is there the potential for installing solar photovoltaic panels? These generate electricity which can be used to run appliances and lighting.
- Are you in an area where you might be able to put a micro wind turbine on your house? You can feed any surplus back into the national grid and get paid for it.

- Feed-in Tariffs (FITs) became available in Great Britain in April 2010. Under this scheme, energy suppliers make regular payments to householders and communities who generate their own electricity from renewable or low carbon sources such as solar electricity (PV) panels or wind turbines.
- Visit the Energy Saving Trust website to find out about a wide variety of grants and discounts available. There is a great online tool to help determine what the best offers are for you, based on your location, type of property and circumstances.

www.energysavingtrust.org.uk

I'm not claiming to be a devoted environmentalist, and, in your case, it doesn't matter whether you're driven by the desire to be green or make a profit. The end result is that the resale value of your home will be far higher if its environmental impact is lower.

37

With or without prejudice

The property game is full of hand-me-down advice, and frankly, most of it is utter rubbish. However, here are a few of my favourite cliché-busting pieces of wisdom:

Service charges can add value

Sounds crazy, doesn't it? But it's true. Although people are often scared off by service charges, they can actually bring added value to your property. For instance, let's say that you're thinking of buying a flat, but the vendor has disclosed that the next year's service charge is going to be an extra £10,000 because of major works. Plenty of people would be put off by this, so the vendor may have to drop his price. This means that you can now buy the flat for less, even with the extra one-off payment. If the flat will be worth £10,000 more with the work done, then go for it.

Another way to view the service charge is to add the cost into the calculation for your mortgage. You'd be surprised at how you can end up with more space than you might have otherwise, for the same money. Let me give you an example. If you were looking to buy a two-bedroom flat up to £400,000, you may be able to buy a three-bedroom flat for £380,000 with a £2,500 per annum service charge. This may put a lot of buyers off, but I think it's great value. You're buying a bigger property for less money. The money saved on a mortgage payment will have to be paid out in the annual service charge, but for the same annual outlay, you're getting more. Over time, with tenants taking more control over the running of their block, the service charge may well reduce. Alternatively, the money may be put to very good use, enhancing the value of your flat.

However, do be careful, check your figures and make sure you're getting value for money. Get a surveyor or your solicitor to check the lease agreement before purchasing. I am not suggesting that you rush out and buy the flat with the most outrageous service charge.

If you are the vendor and want to ensure you get a premium price for your property, you can always suggest to a buyer that you will pay the service charge excess or even the service charges for the next year or so.

Short leases can be a bargain

At one time, you couldn't get a mortgage on a property with less than 70 years left on the lease. But since the introduction of the Commonhold and Leasehold Reform Act 2002, some leaseholders now have the right to buy their own freehold or lease extension at 'a fair price'.

Here, very broadly, is how it works: you buy a flat with a 50-year lease for £200,000. On a long lease it would be worth, say, £230,000. After two years you can buy a lease extension for half the marriage value – i.e. 50 per cent of £30,000. (Please note: determining the cost of the lease extension is worked out using a much more detailed formula and process, but just to give you an idea, and because most times I have come across it, it always seems to end up as about half the marriage value, I thought I'd include this detail.)

So that is an extra £15,000 you have to pay, making your total outlay £215,000 for a flat worth £230,000.

Every lease extension is different. I would highly recommend you visit the Leasehold Advisory Service before snapping up any bargain properties with a short lease. They're a government-funded body, providing free advice on the law affecting residential leasehold and commonhold property in England and Wales. They also offer a mediation service. If you have concerns or issues relating to leasehold property, this website is your starting point.

www.lease-advice.org

Looking down from my balcony I see buyers running away from short leases and high service charges, vendors becoming more and more desperate, and yet a lot of solvable problems, with huge financial gain, if people would just look beyond the end of their nose. Now here's an idea...If you're the vendor of this flat with a 50-year lease, and have owned the property for more than two years, why don't you apply for the lease extension yourself? Find out if you can assign it to any buyer and how much it will cost. Better still, purchase the lease extension prior to putting the property on the market!

Top-floor flats are the most vulnerable to burglaries

Most of us believe that ground-floor flats are the most vulnerable to break-ins or burglaries. However, a police officer once explained to me that top-floor flats are actually the most vulnerable. The reason is, burglars know that property windows, in general, are pretty secure, so the best point of entry is the front door. A break-in to a ground-floor flat is the most likely to be seen, with other people coming in and out of the block, whilst the top floor is the least likely to be seen, with far fewer people going up there.

Buying off-plan is always a bargain

Over the years, buying a property before the first brick has even been laid, has been a profitable and popular route for many a thrifty purchaser or investor. However, things can, and do, go wrong.

Buying off-plan can be worth the risk. However, think about the following before pursuing this further:

1. Is the property properly priced? Compare it to other similar new-build developments, as well as similar-sized properties in the area.

2. Do you really want to live in the new-build area? Just to bag a bargain?

3. There is no certainty, or history, with your new neighbours – and often off-plan developments attract investors who will be placing tenants right next door. Are you comfortable with this? Have adequate sound-proofing measures been taken by the developer?

4. Who *is* the developer and are they well established? Can they afford to complete the development if times turn for the worse? Are they registered with the National House-Building Council (NHBC)? If so, this will mean they're insured.

5. Finally, think about how long you intend to live in the new-build property – and what supply will be like when you come around to selling. Are there 20 new-build developments, with hundreds of apartments all on top of one another, within a small area? Are they of quality build? Are there communal areas or unique features which will set your new-build apart from other nearby developments? This will impact on the demand, and ultimately, the price you'll achieve when selling.

There are plenty more so-called truisms that people trot out in the property world. All I am saying is, a canny operator does not fall for old wives' tales, and nor should you.

38

Be diligent

As a buyer, you must be diligent and treat the purchase as a business transaction. Don't take anyone's word for anything. Remember, the vendor wants his house sold, the agent wants his commission, your friends and family don't want to offend you, or may lack an understanding of the property market. Even the surveyor gets paid regardless of your decision. Your solicitor is the only one who is truly on your side. That is, if they're any good.

I'm not saying that you shouldn't trust anyone involved in the process – just that you need to clarify the accuracy of their story.

Get physical evidence and proof to back up your queries. If an estate agent tells you the property has working fireplaces, check to see if this is so. If you're not sure how, have someone else do the job for you.

If the vendor tells you the run-down council estate on the corner of your street is being demolished, phone the local council to confirm.

Yes, under the Property Misdescriptions Act, an estate agent must inform a buyer of any significant matter relating to the property – but neither the agent nor the vendor are qualified builders and may not be aware that the sticky door in the bathroom is due to subsidence.

Friends and family will often react to a property with their needs in mind – not yours. Perhaps they have a large family and enjoy an open-plan kitchen/living space to socialise and interact with their children. They'll be mortified by the small kitchen and the layout of the home with the reception at the other end of the property (which works perfectly well for your needs).

Constructive criticism is well worth listening to, but keep in mind that their opinions may be biased.

At the end of the day, it's really down to you. Use the Internet, it can be your best friend. And use professional help to assist with the technical aspects of the sale. In Chapters 51 through to 55, I will outline the absolute importance of surveyors and solicitors in the buying process and how best to use their services. The final decision to buy, however, and the consequences of that decision, lie solely in your hands.

39

Quizzing
the vendors

At this stage you will probably have dozens of questions for the vendor on a whole range of issues, such as local schools, shops and the closest restaurants. However, there are other key questions to ask, in the nicest possible way, of course!

How long have they lived there?

Moving is such an arduous and stressful task that no one would do it unless they had to. Therefore, be cautious if the vendors are moving after less than a year in the property, with no good reason. Could there be hidden problems?

Why are they selling?

If the vendors avoid eye contact or mumble when you ask, be suspicious. Sure, people move on for positive reasons like new jobs and extending families, but they also move for plenty of concerning reasons, too.

What are the neighbours like?

Watch out for tight-lipped smiles or a knowing glance between spouses on this one. Be aware that if the vendors have made any sort of formal complaint about a neighbour, either to the police, the council, or other agencies such as mediation services, then it is illegal for them not to declare the fact. Your solicitor will also ask this question during the conveyancing process.

If the vendors say nothing and, at a later stage, problems arise – perhaps noisy dogs or out-of-control kids – you can take legal action against them.

Much harder to discover, though, are the less serious but still potentially irritating problems, such as a neighbour addicted to late-night horror movies with the volume at full blast.

Whatever the vendor's response, mention that you plan on talking to the neighbours, just to get a feel for the area, this may prompt more information.

What kind of property are they moving to, and where?

Is it to another area or to a larger property? Or is it to a similarly sized property a short distance away? Their answer could be revealing.

40

Probing the vendors

By this stage, you may be feeling like a detective, with all these questions and subtle ploys, but you cannot relax yet – you still have more questions for the vendors.

These three questions are designed to help you make the final decision on whether to proceed or not, and how much to offer.

It is possible that the vendor's agent will already have given you this information, but if not, do not proceed without it. And in any case, the vendors might be more likely to divulge some useful snippets.

> *It really is an expensive process isn't it… We just paid £x for our survey. I'd be interested to know if I paid over the odds for it. Has anyone else had a survey on this house?*

If the answer is 'yes', you might be in a race.

> *Such a lovely house! I can't believe I'm the first to have made an offer. Have you been let down by a previous buyer? Isn't it awful when that happens?*

Again, if the answer is yes, why did the previous buyer back down? Did they know something you don't?

Well I think I have everything I need, but is there anything else – even the tiniest thing – that I should know about the property? It's not that I won't put in an offer, it's just that I'm the sort of person who likes all the bad news up front. I'd feel terrible if I had to pull out of the deal at a later date and let everyone down…

Don't feel sheepish about probing for this kind of information. The vendor's responses could be crucial, for three reasons:

1. Depending on what you hear, you may be alerted to problems that the agent has not mentioned.

2. You may save money by being in the knowledge seat and putting in a lower offer.

3. You will demonstrate to the vendor that you are a serious buyer.

41

Schmoozing the vendors

As you come towards making an offer, it's important for the vendors to like you and to have them on side. It's always much harder for the vendor to get into fierce negotiations with likable buyers.

However much you may detest the vendors as people, or despise their taste in interior décor, never lose sight of the fact that it is in your best interest to maintain a good working relationship with them, for as long as it takes for the sale to complete.

Once you've got the keys, you can sneer at their wallpaper or their personal habits to your heart's content. Until then, be friendly.

Remember, also, that vendors often respond to would-be buyers in an emotional way. Particularly if they are bidding a fond farewell to a longstanding family home and there are other buyers waiting in the wings. They might well decide to sell to someone they like, rather than someone who appears to be an unsuitable future guardian of their beloved home.

Being friendly should make it easier for you to make repeat visits, with your family or children, or to call by to measure up for carpet. Whatever the reason for your visit, use the occasion to let the vendor know how much you're looking forward to moving ahead with the sale and that you will do everything in your power to complete the sale on time.

Once an offer is accepted, keep them up to speed with regular updates on progress with solicitors or conveyancers. Additionally, make sure they know as soon as possible if there are any hiccups in the process. Develop a relationship whereby you're both working together to solve problems, rather than fighting against each other.

Most importantly, to avoid misunderstandings, confirm all details in writing whenever appropriate.

42

Probing the agent

If, after gently probing the vendors, you are still unsure on one or two things, don't hesitate to go back to the vendor's agent and ask the same questions in a more direct fashion.

For example:

- Have any offers been refused?
- Has anyone else had a survey?
- Have there been any abortive sales? If so, why?
- What price do you think the vendor will accept?
- Are there any reasons not to buy this property?

You may wish to preface your questions with a comment similar to the one you put to the vendors, namely: 'I know these are difficult questions for an agent because of the Property Misdescriptions Act, I'm just not very good with surprises and I'd hate to pull out later and let everyone down.'

Under the Property Misdescriptions Act, the agent has to answer all of these questions truthfully. Even verbally, a lie could lead to you prosecuting them.

43 Final questions prior to offering

So you've become firm friends with the vendors and the agents, and are content with all of their responses to your persistent probing. Now it's time to get down to the nitty-gritty. Here are key issues to resolve:

- What time period for exchange are the vendors seeking?
- What time period are they looking for on completion?
- How negotiable is the price?

Don't react or say anything until these questions have been answered. Re-emphasise that you're just doing your homework and will be submitting an offer shortly.

What are the exact boundaries and details of the property?

Obtain a site plan from the Land Registry or your solicitor, and check all the boundaries with your future neighbours. Also, get a lease plan and check that all the accommodation and storage rooms on the particulars are listed and correct. Be sure to ask about any disputes over ownership.

What fixtures and fittings are included in the sale?

Whatever you agree upon, this will form part of your contract with the vendor. Some vendors like to take everything with them, from the carpet to the light bulbs (honestly!), whereas others are happy to start afresh in their new place. You may have to negotiate an extra sum for the items you want, or they may throw them in to seal the deal. Either way, you should draw up and agree a detailed inventory that forms part of the contract.

Who is the vendor's solicitor?

Make a note of their name and contact details. This will be useful if, for example, you discover that the vendor is talking to another buyer. In this case, you can get your solicitor to speak to their solicitor, one professional to another.

Now stop talking and go home.

It's not time to offer just yet.

44

Suss the market and don't be silly

So now you've really done the legwork and asked all the necessary questions. You've found a property you like, even if it does have an avocado bathroom suite, and now it's crunch time. How much are you going to offer?

My first recommendation, as you might expect, is to ask the estate agent for advice. Ask him or her to provide data on at least three homes that have recently sold in the neighbourhood. Calculate the difference between the original list price and the final price of the homes sold.

If the average sale price is, say, 5 per cent below the asking price, then you may conclude that you can make an offer on your chosen property of 8–10 per cent below the asking price. That way you will leave yourself a little room to negotiate.

Another factor to consider is whether the trend in recent home sales is up or down. For instance, if a year ago homes were selling for 10 per cent below list price, but recent properties are going at 3 per cent below, then you might want to tighten your opening bid to just 5 per cent below asking price.

Above all, be very careful about making silly offers. If you are really determined to buy the property, don't lowball just for the sake of it.

You may have been told the worst thing that can happen with a really low offer is that the vendor will say 'no', but this is nonsense. A silly offer will not only make you look daft, but the vendor will also lose confidence in you as a buyer, and may not want to deal with you anymore.

Even if you then increase your offer to a sensible amount, the vendor may have good grounds to wonder whether you might try a similar stunt further down the line and reduce your price at a crucial moment.

Before being tempted to make a low offer, step onto the balcony and put yourself in the shoes of the vendor. How does your behaviour seem? Would you like to do business with someone who seems to be a player, who changes their mind, and who might, in the long run, not prove to be reliable? Now revise your offer.

45 Before you make your final offer

Here's a final checklist of things you should have done before working out your offer:

Checklist

☐ You have spoken to local agents.

☐ You have looked at the prices of comparable properties.

☐ You have spoken to local shopkeepers and to neighbours.

☐ You have contacted the Land Registry or checked their website.

☐ You have worked out the value of the property in £ per square feet and compared the value to other properties you like.

☐ You have analysed the vendor's motives for moving.

☐ You have understood the reasoning behind their asking price.

☐ You have gleaned as much information as you can from the agent.

Your Balcony Form

Have you filled in as much of your Balcony Form as possible? On it you should have written the price you want to pay for the property, why you feel that it's the right price in its present condition, and included any special potential you think it might have.

On your Balcony Form you should have also considered any compromises that would aid a successful outcome. Have you established all the various justifications and circumstances under which the vendors may accept a lower offer? For example, if contracts were exchanged in, say, 48 hours, or if completion took place in 10 days.

Nearly there…
What about questioning yourself?

1.   Would you, as the buyer, pay a little more if you could have more of the property's contents?

2.   Would you pay more if you could move in sooner, or have a longer completion period?

3.   Would you pay more if the vendor allowed you to carry out work on the property between exchange and completion?

46

Back to the balcony

So, you're about to put in an offer. All parties seem willing to proceed, and by now you can't bear the thought of anyone else owning it. STOP right there!

Step out onto the balcony, take a deep breath, and answer the following questions as honestly as you can. If you are buying with a partner or a group of friends, make sure they are either on the balcony with you, or do your best to answer honestly on their behalf.

Remember, this crucial stage in the process may find you at your most vulnerable.

Questions for the balcony:

Is this really the right property, or are you just fed up with the process?

Are you being pressurised into a decision by the other parties?

How much is the property really worth?

Still happy to proceed? Go for it!

47

How to behave

How many times have I heard buyers say, 'I'm going to beat them down on the price, I was brilliant at bargaining in the souk on our last holiday!'? Well yes, I'm sure you were fantastic at bargaining over a piece of £20 pottery, but that's not the same as negotiating the biggest purchase of your life. Believe me, I've negotiated thousands of property sales, and I know.

Here's some advice:

Be clever

Whenever you think the moment is right, casually ask the agent what price he or she thinks the vendor will accept. Don't tell them you are about to make an offer. Just say you want a rough idea. You will be amazed at what nuggets sometimes come out! I once heard an agent let slip, 'Oh I'm sure my colleague mentioned the vendor was thinking of taking £30,000 off the price'. Suddenly you could have found a bargain.

Don't be silly

Sorry to repeat myself, but as I advised earlier, playing so-called 'hardball' rarely works. The deals which go through with the fewest problems are those in which everyone trusts each other from the start.

Consider only the facts

By all means make an offer below the asking price, but you must justify this by backing it up with information. Base your offer on as many facts as you can. For instance:

- The neighbouring house sold for £x.
- A nearby flat sold for £y and was in much better condition.
- It will cost you £z to bring this property up to scratch.
- The press and the building societies say the market is going in which direction?
- You are getting an 80 per cent mortgage and cannot extend to a larger deposit.
- The buyer of your property has reduced their offer price.

Never let emotion influence the amount you are prepared to offer.

Put a deadline on it

When it comes time to communicate your offer, it's wise to put a deadline on it. You certainly want to give the vendor enough time to consider your offer, but you don't want to leave it open-ended. You want a decision. And, the longer it's left, the higher the chance of a better offer coming in from another buyer. I find that 48–72 hours is sufficient time for a vendor to consider their options and if this is not possible, just extend the deadline (you don't have to change the price offered).

48

Putting up your offer

In a perfect world, if you've built up a great rapport with the vendor, I'd put the offer up boldly, face-to-face. Have with you all the facts as to why you're offering the price you are. Chapter 50 covers this style of negotiation in further detail.

If, however, it's not practical to meet with the vendor in person, there is nothing wrong with speaking with the agent over the phone to submit your offer. Follow the golden rules for offering, outlined below, and confidently state that 'due to reasons x, y and z, you've thought about it and you'd like to offer £x'. Then, don't say a word and listen to the response. It will tell you the most.

If the response is lethargic, it's likely the agent knows the vendor's minimum acceptable price, and your offer doesn't meet it.

If their response is excitable, the deal is likely to be agreed.

If you're a nervy person, or anxious about putting up the offer, think beforehand about what the likely outcomes could be from your discussion with the agent or vendor. Go up on the balcony, prepare, and write on cards what your response to each outcome would be.

If the agent says, 'sounds great, let me speak to the owner. If it's not enough will you be prepared to offer more?' you'll be ready to respond with a clear mind.

Golden rules for submitting an offer

1. Before you mention the price you're willing to offer, explain your background, circumstances and the homework you've done.

2. Talk about the time frame you can work within.

3. Offer your price.

4. Shut up and listen for their reaction. It will tell you a lot.

5. If the agent asks whether you would be prepared to pay more, sound negative and doubtful.

6. Follow up your conversation with an email, which you should have written before you phoned as a way of composing all your research and reasonings (but not sent). The reason to send the email is so that, not only is it in writing, but also, with a bit of luck, the agent will forward it on to the owners (with all of your detailed, and delicately phrased justifications).

7. Get out onto the balcony and breathe in the fresh air.

49

I repeat, do not blabber

On page 40 I advised you not to blabber during the negotiations, under any circumstances, and I meant it. Keeping quiet is essential. Even if you get a phone call out of the blue from a competing estate agent, do not tell them you've made an offer and where you are hoping to buy.

Why not? Well, say you are about to negotiate a great deal; he or she may gazump you. (For more on gazumping, see Chapter 15). Secondly, say this agent also has your hopeful new property listed on his books, and for one reason or another, he didn't show it to you. His boss is going to be furious and so he may try to put you off buying it, or even try to sell it to someone else.

Not only should you not tell another agent where you have agreed to buy, but you shouldn't tell anyone until you exchange. You never know who might be listening in the wings with a higher offer.

Finally, NEVER tell the vendor's agent that you might be prepared to increase the price when you make your offer, as he will be obliged to tell the vendor. After all, the vendor is his client, and we agents are paid to get the best possible price. Never forget that this is where our loyalties lie.

So don't blabber. In the property business loose talk can cost money.

50

Face to face

Another successful approach to negotiation is to do so face to face with the vendor. Face-to-face negotiations are always better than dealing with people over the telephone. I agree that it's much easier to call your agent and say, 'Tell the vendor if he doesn't accept my terms he can forget it!' than it is to actually say it to the vendor's face, but you can learn so much more during face-to-face meetings: about a person's reasoning, about their state of mind, and whether in fact you are negotiating over the same thing.

I love this story I found, again, through reading *Getting to Yes: Negotiating Agreement Without Giving In* (see Recommended Reading on page 239). This true story arose during the Strategic Arms Limitation Talks (SALT), between the USSR and the USA during the Cold War. The meetings almost broke down as the Soviets would only give the Americans permission to inspect their weapons three times a year, whilst the Americans were insisting on ten. The talks were at the point of collapse when some bright spark raised the question, 'What exactly is involved in these inspections? Do they last a week or a month?' It turned out the Soviets had thought that each inspection lasted a month, whereas the Americans were thinking one day.

The message is clear. Get face to face and understand the other person's point of view. A face-to-face meeting gives you the chance to appreciate where they're coming from. Really listen, from the balcony, as if you were a third party. Try to find out what their Best Alternative to a Negotiated

Agreement (BATNA) is. That is, if you can't get to an agreement with the vendor on your offer price, what will they do? What are their alternatives?

Are other buyers interested in the property? Are they selling because they *have to*, or just for a change of lifestyle? What is their best alternative to accepting your offer? If the property has been on the market for only a week, and it's a strong market, they may want to wait for the full asking price (your BATNA will never be strong if you are desperate for a specific property in a sellers' market). However, if the property has been on the market for four months, with no other interest, and you've just offered £200,000, whilst they may really need an additional £10,000 to make a profit, do they have the time or funds to hold out for the asking price of £220,000. They could have a bridging loan and there may be a threat of being repossessed. Do they have any other alternative? Can they afford to hold out for that extra £10,000?

Analyse your BATNA, and that of the other party, on page iv. It will increase your negotiating power.

I believe in face-to-face meetings so much that, when an offer is within 10 per cent of an acceptable price, I insist on my negotiators putting all parties together in a meeting. Approximately four out of five times a sale will be agreed.

It also helps in case there are any future disputes. A personal relationship and a 'gentleman's handshake' (excuse the terminology, ladies, I hope you get my point) will assist in solving the dispute enormously. Build up this rapport by listening to the other party's needs, and feed this information back to them to show you understand. Also, during the process, call them often and keep them updated with what is going on.

51

Surveying
the surveys

Congratulations. Your offer has been accepted and approved by the lender, subject to survey and solicitors checks. Now it really is time to get serious.

So what's a survey? And when is a survey *not really* a survey? People are often confused by the different kinds of surveys available, and believe that a building society valuation will point out problems within the property. This is definitely not the case. It will only tell the lender whether or not the house is worth the money asked for it. Given the huge range of problems that can affect a property, amazingly, around 80 per cent of all homebuyers still rely on the valuation report rather than paying for a more detailed survey.

These are the three main levels of survey:

Mortgage Valuation Report

Your lender will insist on this before approving your loan. The report will take into account such factors as the condition and age of the house, the area, and what comparable properties are selling for locally. But that's all.

If you're buying a relatively new property that's still under a reputable builder's warranty, such as a NHBC guarantee, you can probably get away with just a valuation report. However, it won't give you any bargaining power when it comes to the deal.

Normally you have to pay the cost of this valuation (around £450, although it can get more expensive for bigger, pricier properties). However, your lender may refund this cost when the mortgage is finalised. Some lenders will offer a free mortgage valuation as part of the package to attract your custom.

The RICS HomeBuyer Report

Previously a Homebuyers' Survey and Valuation Report (HSVR or HSV), the HomeBuyer Report (HBR) follows a standard format and gives you an overview of the condition of the property, rating the structural condition of the building and pointing out any major or minor defects and conditions. It will also tell you whether the purchase price is reasonable and the surveyor's opinion on reinstatement costs (you will need this for insurance purposes). However, the property is only inspected on a fairly superficial level (for example, wiring, drainage and gas are not covered).

If you're buying a typical house or flat, of conventional construction and in reasonable condition, a HBR may well suffice. It's designed to help you make a reasoned and informed decision on whether or not to go ahead with buying the property. Approximate cost is up to £750.

Building Survey

Formerly known as a Structural Survey, this is the most detailed report and, in my opinion, a necessity for any house that's unusual or over 75 years old. The surveyor will report on the construction, the state of the walls, foundations, roof, plumbing, wiring, heating and woodwork. You may also specify other factors for inspection. You will receive a written report outlining any potential problems and need for future maintenance. Some surveyors also provide a video record.

The cost of the survey will depend on the age, size and condition of the property, but will be from £1,000 upwards. Most lenders won't quote for this as they would instruct a local surveyor with whom you, as the buyer, would agree a fee. Also, as the whole building needs to be inspected, a building survey is usually best carried out on houses rather than flats.

The best solution as a buyer is to have your basic mortgage valuation carried out by your lender and then an independent Home Buyers or Building Survey conducted by a registered surveyor who is a member of the Royal Institution of Chartered Surveyors (RICS). Sometimes the lender will let you use the same surveyor for both, which can result in some fee savings.

52

Choosing
a surveyor

Like solicitors and estate agents, not all surveyors are the same. It's well worth doing some research to make sure you find the best around. Ask friends, family and colleagues who have bought a property recently if they can recommend anyone.

If you have trouble sourcing a reliable recommendation, make sure you choose a local surveyor. They will have a better knowledge of specific problems in the locality, as well as having their finger on the pulse in regards to local property values.

Also make sure your surveyor belongs to the Royal Institution of Chartered Surveyors (RICS). You can search the RICS website (www.rics.org/uk) to find a surveyor close to you or your intended property.

If the proposed purchase is an unusual type of construction, make sure they have expertise in this area.

If possible, choose a surveyor who is on the panel of the building society providing your mortgage. If so, they will be able to conduct the mortgage valuation at the same time as the survey, saving you money.

Ask them how long they estimate it will take to get the report to you. Does that time period match your needs?

Finally, don't use a surveyor recommended by your estate agent. I'm not questioning a surveyor's professionalism, all I'm saying is that it's harder for them to be totally objective about a property when the client was introduced by a friend, relying on their commission.

53

Getting the most from your surveyor

Once you've chosen your surveyor you will need to instruct him or her to carry out the work.

Make sure you give your instructions in writing, and detail any areas that are of concern to you (such as damp patches or cracks).

Ask if you can go around the property with them at the end of the inspection. It will give you a much better idea of the situation. During this time, you can ask them for clarification on everything, and to explain any areas you don't understand.

When you get the report, it will contain conclusions under headings such as Condition Ratings (for the materials, construction, services, fixtures and fittings and so on), Issues for your Legal Advisors, Risks, Valuation and more. Get them to talk you through these.

If there is a legal problem which suddenly crops up in the survey (for instance, an extension built without permission), talk to your solicitor immediately.

Ask the surveyor to give you some idea of the cost of rectifying any problems they discover.

Don't be alarmed by any problems thrown up in the survey; in most cases they can be remedied. You could, in any case, use this information to bargain down the price, if it uncovered problems the vendors weren't aware of, or that you hadn't taken into account when making your offer.

Like every professional, surveyor's written reports will tend to err on the side of caution. Indeed, you want them to be as pessimistic as possible in their written report. However, if you want a more balanced or off-the-record view, it's better to have a chat on the phone.

Your three main questions for the surveyor should be:

1. Is the property mortgageable?

2. What major expense is the property likely to entail over the next five years?

3. Is it value for money?

Finally, don't be afraid to get a second opinion. If Surveyor A suggests there are things wrong with the property, and the vendor disagrees, how do you know who to believe? Surveyors can get it wrong and vendors want to sell their property. Yes, you may have already spent close to £3,000 on legal and survey fees, but, if it looks like the deal on your dream property is going down the drain, why not spend an extra £750 on another survey for peace of mind? Or split the cost with the vendor. Either way, you want to be certain.

54

Choosing
a solicitor

The role of the solicitor (or conveyancer) is to validate and project manage the property transaction through to completion. The word 'conveyancing' means that the property will be 'conveyed' or transferred from one person to another. In England and Wales you can use a licensed conveyancer instead of a solicitor. They offer the same service, but are solely limited to property transactions.

Having a good estate agent is beneficial, and having a good surveyor is essential, but, at the end of the day, they both have a product to sell. A clever solicitor I know once compared his role in the process to the equivalent of border security at an airport – acting on behalf of your best interests and making sure nobody pulls the wool over your eyes. The solicitor ensures the seller hasn't accidentally left out any important information and that all of your queries are resolved. Therefore, finding the right one for you is crucial.

There's nothing more stressful than a solicitor who appears to be dragging his or her feet, holding up the whole buying/selling process. You want someone who is efficient, fast and likely to oversee your transaction with the least possible hassle. The last thing you want is some pedantic slow coach (or someone inexperienced at conveyancing) who might jeopardise the sale by holding things up.

If you have a family or business solicitor with whom you're happy, check they're also experienced at conveyancing. Remember, this is a specialist area of law, and a tax specialist or family law expert may not always be the best person to handle your property transaction.

A personal recommendation from someone who has just bought a house is one of the best ways to find a solicitor.

The Law Society can also offer help and advice when looking for a suitable solicitor:

www.lawsociety.org

All solicitors in private practice must hold a practicing certificate issued by the Solicitors Regulation Authority. This certificate guarantees that the solicitor is qualified to practice and has insurance to protect you if anything goes wrong.

If you want to be sure, contact the Solicitors Regulation Authority, or use the 'find a solicitor' tool on The Law Society website.

Find out what the solicitor's services cover and what they can do for you. Will you get on? Speak to them in person to find out. Choose a local solicitor, as like with a local surveyor, they'll be more in tune with local councils and common issues relating to the types of properties found in the area.

55

Getting the most from your solicitor

Fees for conveyancing work can vary widely, so always get several quotes from solicitors and/or conveyancers.

Check what's included in the quote. Be wary of a solicitor offering a suspiciously low quotation. It usually means they are likely to spend less time on your case and/or hand over the detail to an unqualified assistant. Buying a property is not the time to squabble over a few hundred pounds. Understand the importance of *good* advice and ensure you go for a solicitor who will give you value for money. As a guide, it would be difficult to do a thorough job for under £800.

Make sure you get a detailed quote in writing (as solicitors must do), which will also set out the costs of disbursements (such as the Land Registry fee, stamp duty, and so forth).

Check that they're accredited by the Law Society.

Ask if the solicitor makes full use of the Law Society's National Conveyancing Transaction Protocol. It is a good way of speeding up the conveyancing process, using easy-to-understand standard forms and paperwork relating to fixtures and fittings, title deeds, a property information form, and so on.

Over 90 per cent of transactions involving the Law Society's 5,500 solicitor firms licensed for conveyancing use this Protocol in whole or in part, giving clarity to the process.

In order to get the most from your solicitor, you've got to give them a fair chance. Upon instruction, outline the time frame you want them to work to, how often you'd like to communicate, and what kind of client you are. For example, you might want to leave them alone to get on with the job, only speaking at the time of exchange. Or, you might want a detailed explanation of every query raised during the process.

As with your estate agent and every other party involved in the deal, be sure to develop a good personal relationship with your solicitor; be open about your needs and stay in touch when you've said you would, to maintain the momentum on the deal. This will ensure a stress-free and successful outcome.

From the balcony, watch the nervous purchaser, hesitant to phone and chase his agitated, busy solicitor. He has not slept all night, worried about his purchase. His solicitor is unapproachable and makes him feel like he knows nothing, so why did he choose him when he felt this on day one? It's incredible that he is paying this solicitor to leave his important queries unanswered. From the balcony, you must wonder why someone would choose to instruct a professional they did not warm to and feel was unapproachable on day one.

56

Sold...not!

Just because you've made a successful offer, and the property is considered Under Offer, doesn't mean it is yours, or *Sold*. Similarly, just because someone says they are a cash buyer doesn't mean that they actually have the cash.

Many buyers who have their offer accepted on a property complain when it remains on the market (i.e. For Sale). I understand their concern, but, there is a reason. As mentioned previously, seven out of 10 sales fall through because one of the parties change their mind, or their circumstances alter. So, let's be even-handed about this, and say that, out of the seven sales which fall through, at least half are the buyer's fault.

So with three-and-a-half out of every 10 aborted sales (35 per cent) falling through due to issues on the buyer's side, is it any wonder that sellers want to keep the 'For Sale' sign up, even once they've received the offer? They are naturally nervous that the sale might fall through.

I will admit, yes, some vendors may be unscrupulous, and are keeping the board up in the hope of a better offer (see gazumping, Chapter 15). That's why you shouldn't get too carried away once your offer is accepted. It doesn't count until contracts are exchanged.

Now is not the time to be arranging meetings with interior decorators or buying new furniture. Instead, consider a conversation with the vendor about entering into a goodwill agreement, i.e. The Goodwill Charter (Chapter 15).

Sometimes things do go wrong, so as a minimum, aim for a moral commitment on the sale from the vendor. And keep your fingers crossed.

57

How to win a contract race – and when not to enter

Once you've made your offer, a number of things can happen. Hopefully, if you've developed the right kind of relationship with the vendor and agent, and offered a realistic price, your offer will be accepted. On other rare occasions, the vendor may have two or more interested buyers, putting you all in a 'contract race'. That is, the first to send a deposit and a signed contract gets the house.

It's not a pleasant scenario. The vendor wants you to jump through all the hoops of surveys, mortgage offers and solicitors, and then, at the end of all that, you still might lose the race.

A contract race usually only happens when prices are rising fast or houses are in short supply. They are a sort of informal auction, and only one person can win. The loser is going to end up with a full set of costs and no house.

Ask yourself:

- Do I really want the property enough to put myself through this?
- Is the property realistically priced?
- Is there any real chance of winning?
- How advanced am I with organising the mortgage?
- Is my solicitor quick enough?

Let's just go up on the balcony for a moment and look down. Everyone loves the story of the tortoise and the hare...about the tortoise coming from behind and winning the race. But there weren't abundant legal and survey costs, or emotional turmoil as the tortoise set out. If you were an outsider looking in, would you say that you, the buyer, had a realistic chance of winning? If you knew you had only one week to get into a position to exchange contracts, and there was a large, non-refundable fee, would you still want to enter the race?

As a general rule, you need to be in a position to sign within 10 days. If you and your team can't achieve that, the chances are you will lose. But, if you are still up for it, take the following steps:

- Do not put your solicitor in touch with the vendor's solicitor. According to Law Society rules, if a vendor's solicitor knows his client is in negotiations with a potential *second* buyer, he has to notify the first buyer. You don't want the other buyer to know he is in a race. Cruel, but there it is. The other buyer will of course find out soon enough, but in a race, every hour counts.
- Instruct your solicitor to carry out a search on the property. Tell him he doesn't have to wait for a full written report. He can get a slightly inferior one done by hand, and you can always take out insurance against there being something of

significance between the two. This is called a personal search, and you will need to check that your lender will accept this.

- An organised vendor will retain copies of all the correspondence their solicitor has sent out to the other party, such as a copy of the lease and the standard answers to enquires. Getting hold of these will save you time.
- Use couriers, if necessary, to move paperwork around quickly and make sure you're on top of things.
- When you have your mortgage offer in place, your hand-drawn search results and your deposit ready, ask your solicitor to call the vendor's solicitor and carry out what is called an 'attended exchange'. What this means is that your solicitor attends the vendor's solicitor's office in person to discuss the contract and paperwork, face to face. With a bit of luck, they will be able to exchange there and then.

Hopefully, it is only by this stage that the first party gets to hear they are in a contract race. Of course, by then, they don't have time to do anything about it, so bingo! You win.

Hmm, seems a bit ruthless to me. Should I be getting involved in such a race?

Yes, it is totally ruthless, but highly effective for the winner. I do not enjoy contract races, but they only come about as a direct result of the vendor's behaviour, and are allowed under the system of conveyancing in this country.

I may not approve. I am just telling you how to win the race if you decide to take up the challenge.

58 Make it snappy

A contract race is one way for a buyer to speed up the process but, in truth, anyone can buy a property within 24 hours! Yes, you read it correctly. Anyone can buy a property in 24 hours. There are risks attached, but I am going to tell you how to minimise your exposure to the pitfalls.

Although, why attempt this in the first place? The main reason is that it can put you in a position to negotiate a fantastic bargain or grab that dream home which has suddenly come on the market.

This will only work if you have nothing to sell first, and are prepared.

Here's what you have to do:

A speedy exchange

Step 1: As soon as you decide you want to buy a property, get your mortgage offer agreed in principle. Just leave it subject to a survey on the property you eventually want to buy.

Step 2: When the property in question becomes available, obtain the name of the surveyors on the panel of the building society you intend to use, or ask your mortgage broker.

Step 3: Call the surveyor and explain that you wish to employ them privately to walk around and inspect the property. Tell them you want to know whether the property is mortgageable and also ask, if he were acting for the building society, what value would he put on it. Subject to what the surveyor says, you can now make a very grown-up decision as to whether you should exchange without the formal written mortgage offer from the building society. Ask the building society if they will accept the report from your surveyor. He is, after all, on their panel.

Now your risk has really slimmed down to the building society sending in a different surveyor, who values it at less, or that they take too long dealing with the paperwork.

Step 4: To reduce your risk further: on the day you decide to make a move, go to a second building society with your surveyors report, and then see which lender comes up with the formal offer first.

Step 5: Do try and negotiate a contract with your vendor that gives a longer completion if you need it, so if there is a delay you do have time and can get the second building society in to view.

Step 6: Get your solicitor to call the vendor's solicitor and explain that you wish to exchange within 24 hours. Then, ask your solicitor to do one of the following: either they must make an appointment to go to the vendor's solicitor's office, or ask the vendor's solicitor to email over a contract and answer as many of your solicitor's enquiries as they can.

Step 7: Tell your solicitor to do a personal search with the local council rather than a written one (which can take up to three weeks to arrive). The personal search will cost a couple of hundred pounds more, but can prove to be very valuable in the whole scheme of things. There still may be some outstanding queries, which can't be dealt with within this time frame. Don't worry about it. Simply exchange subject to these queries being resolved.

Some solicitors will tell you that you can't exchange within 24 hours, but believe me you can. One advantage is that it locks the vendor into selling to you and stops them selling to someone else.

The benefits of a quick completion

Rather than waiting the normal 28 days, a co-operative building society can allow you to complete in 10 days (and in some cases even less). Telling the vendor you can complete in just 10 days gives you considerable power and will allow you to lever a lot of extras, particularly if they are desperate to sell. If you are in this position, use it for all it's worth. It will also make you sound like a cash buyer.

Do double check your lender will do this before making claims to an excitable vendor.

I would like to point out, I'm not suggesting you proceed with such haste in every property purchase. In fact, don't use this method unless necessary. There are more risks involved, it is more expensive, and you certainly won't make friends with your professional advisors if they're not used to working to such stringent deadlines. Saying this, I have used this approach personally, and advised on it for many a client. And it works.

59 Improvements before completion

On average, there is a four-week period between exchange and completion. So why not put that time to good use in your new property? In fact, if you move quickly enough you can have four weeks' worth of work done on the house before you even move in! Surely that's not possible, I hear you say.

But it is. Depending on the type of renovations and, of course, whether the property is empty or not, the vendor shouldn't mind you using this time to get quotes for work to be carried out, or, if you're super-organised, for the work to commence during this period. If for no other reason, the vendor should be satisfied in knowing that if the sale does fall through, they'll end up with work done on their home at no cost to themselves.

It is a huge benefit to you, the buyer, as between exchange and completion there are no mortgage payments to be made, or a dreadful mess for you to live in whilst major building work commences.

Similarly, if you propose to get some building works done that need planning permission, you can set the wheels in motion before completion. You don't have to own the property, or have the vendor's permission to submit – you will just have to notify the vendor of your application.

If it takes four weeks to exchange and four weeks to complete, an early planning application can save you eight weeks delay on your building works.

60

Before you complete

Here are three actions to carry out in the period between exchange and completion:

1. Check your insurance

Organise your buildings insurance once you've exchanged, and most certainly before you complete. Once the paperwork is done and the house is yours, you are responsible for the insurance (in certain circumstances you can be liable from exchange – check with your insurance broker). Should the house burn down before you've got it organised, tough.

2. Remedial work

Check that any remedial work the vendor has promised to carry out has been completed to your satisfaction.

3. Final inspection

I thoroughly recommend that you view the property again, just prior to completion. Otherwise, you might hand over the money and find that the vendor has taken something out they shouldn't have, or that there is a recent defect that may still be the vendor's responsibility.

I'm sure that in such circumstances your solicitor will say 'you can sue' but, trust me, possession is nine-tenths of the law.

If there is anything missing, you should refuse to go through with the completion until it has been sorted out.

61 Buying without an agent

As I have said, most people buy through an estate agent, as it's all about finding the perfect property. To do this you'll need to see a variety of homes, of which most are listed through agents. There's no fee or cost to the buyer for viewing, making offers or exchanging contracts through an estate agency (the vendor pays the agent the fee in the sale of their property). But, if for some reason, you have an extreme dislike of dealing with agents and you're confident and prepared to put in the extra effort, there is no reason why you cannot buy privately.

There can, of course, be disadvantages to buying these types of listings. Firstly, sellers may think that, because they're not paying an agents' commission, they can demand a higher price. Additionally, they may have an unrealistic expectation of the market value of their property (it's pretty rare for it to work the other way around, i.e. for vendors to be unaware of the true value of their home, allowing you to snap up a bargain).

Here are some ideas and approaches for finding (and seeking) privately listed properties:

The Internet

www.tepilo.com
www.thelittlehousecompany.co.uk
www.houseladder.co.uk
www.houseweb.co.uk
www.gumtree.com
www.loot.com

Please keep in mind that websites such as Rightmove.co.uk, Findaproperty.com and Zoopla.co.uk only advertise properties listed with estate agents.

Private advertisements

Look through the property classifieds in the local newspaper, and place a 'wanted' advert if necessary, with details of the kind of property you're looking for and the price range.

Shop window advertisements

Again, a 'wanted' advert in the local shop window might produce results, especially if you make it clear that you're a private buyer with no chain.

Leafleting

Once you have identified a street (or streets) that you're interested in, why not drop a polite note stating that you're a private buyer and that if anybody is considering moving, could they please contact you. This can be remarkably effective.

Using the local grapevine

Talk to porters in apartment blocks and generally put the word around the neighbourhood. You never know who might have useful inside information.

62 Buying to let

So far we've concentrated on issues facing those wishing to buy or sell a primary dwelling. Before moving on, I'd like to comment on the buy-to-let market. In my experience, few people understand this aspect of the property world. Indeed, several of my contemporaries, with a great deal of experience and knowledge of property, have lost money in buy-to-let.

The biggest mistake in buy-to-let is thinking you'll get a profit on rental income from the start. This emphasis is wrong. What you should be focusing on is the much bigger goal of capital appreciation.

Say you've bought a property at its full market value, and you're planning on a juicy 10 per cent return from the rental income. Sounds good. But what happens if you purchased with 80–90 per cent borrowings, and interest rates go up? Or rental prices go down? Maybe the house also needs some repairs. Then there are 'voids', or gaps between rental periods, and if you are using a letting agent, you'll pay around 10 per cent commission on rent, plus a further 5 per cent on management. See how easy it can be to get into deep water?

So how can you avoid this, if you are still keen on buy-to-let? First, you are better off buying a property at 10 per cent below the market price, with a 6 per cent return, than to pay full market price expecting a 10 per cent return. Should things go pear-shaped, you've bought below market value, and you've got a way out.

Second, don't purchase a buy-to-let with anything higher than 70 per cent borrowings. If you stick at this level, and buy at 10 per cent (or so) below market value, you'll be safe. With these kinds of percentages, if the rent covers your interest and outgoings – give or take a little – you'll be fine. Don't panic if you have to throw in some money for repairs, you have the margin to absorb it.

Remember, your aim is a nice big windfall from capital appreciation.

Third, my advice is to let the property unfurnished. It might take longer to find a tenant, and you will get less rent overall, but they're likely to stay longer (having moved or even purchased furniture, they're less likely to *up-sticks* at short notice), and you will have less voids. Additionally, because it's their furniture and effects they will tend to look after things better, meaning fewer call-outs for you or the managing agents, dealing with problems such as broken televisions, holes burnt in the carpet and so on. In fact, you might be able to cope without a managing agent at all, saving a substantial amount in fees. On top of this, your agent will charge less rental commission in years two and three if the same tenant continues the lease.

Finally, don't fall in love with your investment.

Selling

63 Are you sure you want to sell?

Dumb question, maybe – after all, very few of us can afford not to sell our existing property if we are buying somewhere else. But let's just consider some of the scenarios that we occasionally come across in our offices. You may say, 'Oh, that's not me', but read on all the same. It's always worth paying heed to cautionary tales!

Scenario one

You want to escape the rat race. You want to flee the city. (We meet people like you all the time, particularly in London.) So you sell up and buy a much cheaper place in the country. Heaven at last and pots of money in the bank...

Two years later you are bored silly, and desperate to get back to the big smoke. But your nest egg has diminished and prices have shot up during the interim. You end up in a part of the city you never liked, with a longer commute, in a property that is too small.

Question: could renting out your original property in the city have covered the rental of a place in the country, at least until you were absolutely sure of where you wanted to be?

Scenario two

Your partner is offered a dream position in another city. So you sell up and move, only to find that the job is a nightmare, or you can't stand your new surroundings, or the children aren't settled. Again, renting out your home would have made it far easier to return, or even your partner moving a month or two beforehand, renting a smaller apartment, just to test the waters before uprooting the family on a whim.

Scenario three

Here's a more unusual situation, but true nevertheless. A middle-aged, professional couple living in a large and very beautiful property in central London both lost their jobs within a few months of each other. Dispirited, unable to find new jobs, and with their funds running out, they put their house on the market, thinking they had no other option but to leave London and somehow survive in a cheaper part of the country. By chance, they met a neighbour who was renting out his house to a family from the USA for a surprisingly large monthly rental. So they did the same, and found that the rental income covered all their outgoings, plus the rent on a cheap house in southern France. After a wonderful year abroad they returned to their old house tanned, reinvigorated and ready to start afresh.

64

Stop!
Do not attempt
to move!

We've just looked at some scenarios where it would make more sense to rent than to sell up and move on. Here are a few more situations you might want to consider.

You're not 100 per cent certain you want to move

Sit down with a calculator and work out exactly how much you'll be paying in stamp duty as well as solicitor and agency fees if you sell one house and buy another. It's quite a lot, isn't it? Maybe renting is the smarter option after all.

Paying off your existing mortgage

Did you check there are no redemption penalties payable on your mortgage? If there are, you might be heavily penalised for paying it off before a certain date. In which case, renting a property might be the better option in the meantime.

Consider extending

Sometimes, life throws us googlies when we're least expecting them and before you know it you need more room: elderly parents are suddenly widowed and need to be housed;

pregnancies, planned or otherwise; a redundancy gives you or your partner the chance to change careers and work from home. But the problem is, if it's not a buoyant market, you could be making a significant loss by selling your property. So why not expand instead of moving?

Get an architect or builder in and keep your mind open about the options. Converting the loft or building an extension are the more obvious options, but there are other creative solutions, like losing the garage or splitting big rooms into two.

Sure, you might be living amidst builder's rubble for several months, but in the long run it could be less stressful than moving.

In every case, make sure you do the sums properly. There's no point in spending a fortune on a conversion and getting into debt if moving really is the cheaper option.

Costs include:

- Legal costs.
- Agent fees.
- Selling fees and stamp duty.
- Removal costs.
- Bills to settle and close.
- Buying items to furnish and decorate a new property, as well as buying new fittings and appliances (if you've agreed to leave your existing ones in the home you've just sold).
- Any cost in preparing your house for the new owners.
- Penalties for paying out your mortgage (if applicable).

65

Sell before you buy

It is always better to sell before you buy if you are relying on the equity within the property to fund your next home purchase. You will be in a much stronger position as a cash buyer, having already exchanged on your property, and you'll certainly be taken more seriously.

If you walked into my office and offered the full asking price on a house for sale, without even putting your own property on the market first, as an agent protecting my client's best interests, I would tell the vendor not to accept the offer, or even *think* about accepting it until you had your own property under offer.

If it's a buyers' market, you may have to wait a long time to secure a purchaser, especially at the right price. So, there's not much point in going out spending time looking at houses, setting your heart on a particular property, getting emotionally attached, running up legal and survey fees, only to end up with nothing because you haven't sold your own property first.

If it's a sellers' market, at least you can control the process a little more, and hopefully start to dictate the pace. In these circumstances, you can tell your buyer you will accept their bid, subject to you finding what you want to buy within a given time.

So, regardless of market conditions, always list your home for sale as soon as you can.

Of course, if you manage to sell before you buy, it can be inconvenient to pack up your house and move your belongings into storage or rented accommodation. But, whether this is likely or not, don't get carried away making offers on other homes until yours is under offer.

If you are close to buying before you sell, keep in mind the hidden costs of doing so:

- You will possibly be paying off two mortgages until your home is sold.
- You'll be stung for two lots of council tax as well as insurance on two properties.
- You'll need funds available to cover the legal costs on your purchased property.
- Without the proceeds of your sale, you'll also need to cover stamp duty (which can add up to six to twelve months of additional mortgage payments).

Here's a tip: when exchanging on your own house, agree a six-month completion clause, but with the proviso that you can give notice to bring it forward, with say, four weeks' notice. This is called a stop date, and it may give you the best of both worlds... you'll always get a better deal not being in a chain, and you may not have to move into a temporary home either! It gives the buyer satisfaction in knowing they've secured your property and you the satisfaction of knowing your exact financial position and time frames for purchase.

If there is any likelihood of you having to buy and sell properties simultaneously, I would recommend you see a financial broker to discuss your options. To find a local, regulated financial advisor near you, search on the Financial Services Authority website:

www.fsa.gov.uk

66 Preparation, preparation, preparation

Hopefully, by reading this chapter you will realise the number one requirement for selling your property is motivation. As the seller, there is a lot of involvement and effort required to ensure you actually *sell* your property. Being motivated and carrying out a number of the below actions can make the sale of your property run much smoother. If you manage all the following, you can reduce the time it takes to exchange contracts by half.

Deeds and searches

Before you put your property on the market, it is in your best interest to instruct a solicitor. One of the tasks you can have them perform is to make the deeds and searches available. The buyer normally pays for these searches, and there is absolutely no reason why you cannot ask them to reimburse you for the outlay you have effectively made on their behalf. The benefit is that it saves a three- to four- week period when the sale is agreed, the stage at which the buyer normally arranges for these searches.

Prepare a draft contract

Put together a file with your property details, together with a copy of the lease, building insurance details and any service charge information you may have. You can always get copies from the managing agents. Add to this file copies of any household guarantees you may have such as central heating, damp proofing, etc., and send the whole package to your solicitor. They can start to prepare the draft contract so that, as soon as the buyer comes along, the sale can go straight ahead.

Survey

For a relatively modest fee, you will no doubt be able to get a registered surveyor to have a look around your home before you put it on the market. The purpose is not to have a detailed written report, or a document by which to sue the surveyor if they get the value wrong by £5,000. Remember, it's an informal walk-around and they won't be following the detailed, and expensive protocol. All you want to know is if there is anything materially wrong with your property that will impact on the sale – or if a buyer is just trying it on (see following chapter).

Land Registry: www.landregistry.gov.uk

To help establish the value of your property, visit the Land Registry website to find out how much houses that are similar to yours, in neighbouring areas, have sold for on the open market. Note, however, that Registry information does not list the three most recent months of data, so will be a little behind in prices.

Development potential

Does your property have any potential for development – for example, by converting it into flats, or by building in the garden? If so, it will be worth considerably more if sold with planning permission already in place. It could be worth inviting a local architect around to consider the possibilities.

Fixtures and fittings

Prepare in advance an inventory of what you expect to leave; you can always add to it later. You may find your agent refers to this list as part of the Sellers Information Form. However it's labelled, at least would-be buyers will be clear as to what the deal entails.

Get dirty

Once you're done with all the paperwork, it's time to start preparing your property for valuations and inspections. It's time to pull out the Marigolds and the feather duster!

So get motivated and organised. Sellers with a genuine need to move on and a high level of motivation tend to see the sale situation in a clearer light. This doesn't mean selling to the first buyer who offers, but it does usually indicate a *fair* offer will be accepted, allowing the vendor to move on with their life nice and quickly.

67 Valuing your home

Before asking the agents around to assess the value of your property, you should employ the services of an independent chartered surveyor. To find one who is not working for a local estate agent, see the Royal Institution of Chartered Surveyors website and use their 'Find a Surveyor' search engine to find one in your local area.

www.rics.org/uk

Ask the surveyor to come and survey your home with the following in mind:

- You want a verbal report only (a written one is more expensive), unless there is a major problem;
- You want their professional opinion on how much the house is worth;
- You want to know if there is anything wrong with the house which might affect its value, or that will be picked up by the purchaser's surveyor and used to bargain down your price.

The price of this verbal report will vary according to the area you live in, and the age and size of the property. However, it will be a lot less than a full survey, possibly in the region of £400–£500. You may find that some surveyors will not be willing to produce such valuation advice as it could incur a substantial liability for the surveyor if the property sells for under their valuation. Keep in mind, and outline to the surveyor, that it's more to make you aware upfront of anything wrong with the house that may impact on the price you receive.

Most surveyors' valuations have a 10 per cent variant in price, so never expect your buyer's surveyor to value your house at the full price for which you have it on the market.

You might be wondering why I'm suggesting you go to the expense of getting an independent valuation survey when you can research house prices online (www.landregistry.co.uk/houseprices) and receive endless free valuations from local estate agents? But it's all about your approach to the sale, and saving you time and money in the long run. If you know the realistic price of the property as well as any potential structural issues before you put it on the market, you won't get hammered by a buyer's surveyor once an offer is in, and risk losing your buyer. This £400–£500 report could save you weeks of further effort, stress and heartache.

Compare the valuation from the independent surveyor with the information you have from the Land Registry and from the Internet on similar properties for sale in your area. You should now be in a position to estimate the sale price of your house to within 5 per cent of its true value.

68 Mystery shopper

Now that you have an idea of your property's value, you should set about finding at least two estate agents to handle the sale (See Chapter 73 for why you should never agree a sole agency agreement). But how do you know which agents to choose?

My belief is that an estate agency is only as good as the negotiators it employs, and that the best way to assess this is to play the role of a 'mystery shopper'. This requires you to visit various estate agencies anonymously to see how their staff treat you. To really judge their level of service, do not admit that you wish to place your property on the market. Instead, pretend that you are a buyer. This will have two main benefits:

- Firstly, it will give you some indication of how good the agent is or is not;
- Secondly, it will tell you what a property is genuinely worth.

Here's one way of playing the mystery shopper.

Tell the agent your friend or relative wants to move into your area. Ask:

- What's available?
- What's been sold recently?
- How much was it sold for?

You can do this over the phone, but you can't beat doing it face to face. This way you can see the agent's manner, how much attention you're getting, and how friendly and organised they are. You can see how they would market *your* property if you choose them to, and, also, gain their unbiased opinion on the value of your house.

Once they've given you particulars of a property they've recently sold in a road you're interested in, find out the number of the house, and how much it sold for. Tell them you'll look at it on your way home. The reason you're going to check up on this is because some agents will say they've sold a property when they haven't.

Go to the house and ask the occupants what the agent was like. Or, if you're too shy, drop a note in. Then consult the Land Registry (Chapter 30) and check if the sale price tallies with what the agent told you.

You might ask if all this effort is really worth it; but think of it this way – if it ends up gaining you an extra £10,000 on the value of your house, then for a few extra hours research, yes, it's definitely worth it.

Now is the time to call in the agents. Don't tell them about the homework or research you've done. This is your opportunity to test their honesty and how well they know their job. Don't forget, there is no reason why they'll be magically able to get more money for your home than your independent surveyor or research told you, so don't be easily flattered. Perhaps they are very keen to impress as they are looking to put extra instructions on their books, or a sales (and marketing) board up in your road.

It doesn't matter if the agents eventually find out that you were mystery shopping them. If you tell them how important it was for you to find the best agent in town, they'll be flattered to have received the call.

69 Whose valuation is it anyway?

We all want to sell property at the highest possible price and buy at the lowest. However, more often than not, and in London especially, we are in a rising market and there is simply not enough property to go around. This is why prices are so high, the way a free market works – supply and demand.

Does it really matter if you sell your house at £200,000 or £300,000 if what you're going to buy is always £50,000 more? The answer, I'm afraid, is 'yes', as the percentage difference just gets bigger and bigger…

Contrary to popular opinion, agents do not club together and decide to increase prices. Many influences include the state of the economy and interest rates, employment opportunities and business projects planned within an area, local knowledge and, of course, the national press – often turning vendors into gung-ho bulls.

For instance, Neighbour A sells his house for £200,000. Neighbour B reads that prices are rising, and also notices a new supermarket being built five minutes down the road. His expectation is now £205,000. There is a shortage of property, so he gets his £205,000, and so on.

So how do you know who to believe on value? Some say that the easiest way to establish value is to do the following:

1.   Study what's currently available to buy, getting a feel for the market.

2. View a specific property and guess as to the absolute minimum and absolute maximum. And then…

3. Simply take the average or midpoint price.

You'll be surprised at how accurate this figure is.

Say you ask three agents to value your property.

> Agent A values it at £700,000
> Agent B values it at £600,000
> Agent C values it at £620,000

So who's right? Using the above easy three-step approach, the average value would equal £640,000 – but what happens when it's *your* property? You want to believe Agent A, but if he's wrong you might end up with your house on the market for too long, and possibly lose the house you want to buy, becoming stressed beyond comprehension during the process.

But why might Agent A be wrong? Maybe he's desperate for instructions in your road. Or, he's new to the area. Or, he might be new to the job. Or, maybe he's just useless.

Whatever you do, don't place too much reliance on advice from friends or family. Nine times out of 10 their advice is going to be either too safe or too cautious. Rather, try to understand the basis on which the three agents have made their valuations. The following chapters will help.

70

What do agents base their valuations on?

Agents base their valuations on three main factors.

Firstly, they should have a pretty good idea of what similar properties are on the market for, and also, what prices they've achieved in sales.

Secondly, their estimate will be based on their gut instincts.

And finally, they might be telling you what they think you want to hear.

Bear in mind that the agent's estimate is just that – it's an estimate. It is not an official valuation against which you can borrow money. Only a survey can fulfil that function.

You want an agent to base their valuation on facts, wherever possible. They should take into consideration the following factors:

Size	Parking
Specification	Aspect and views
Overall condition	Outside space
Presentation	Tenure
Renovation potential	Security
Wow factor	Vendor situation
Location	Market trends and
Transport links	comparables
The street	

So, although you should certainly be guided by the agent's recommendation, the final decision on the price is yours and yours alone. It is up to the agent to carry out your instructions on the asking price.

Be wary of an agent who tries to 'fish' for the price you're looking for. If he or she isn't capable of coming up with their own figure, you shouldn't be doing business with them.

And watch out for the agent setting an unrealistically high price in order to get your business, locking you into a sole agency contract. As you'll read in Chapter 73, sole agency isn't a good idea, and being lured into it in this way is doubly foolish. In a few weeks, when the property hasn't sold, the agent will then undoubtedly lower the price, and you'll still be stuck in a sole agency contract with a useless agent.

On the other hand, if you trust Agent A's valuation, you can always give it a go at the higher price. If you don't achieve it at least you'll know that you tried, and your agent can then reduce it. Remember, it's always easier to come down in price than it is to go up (in fact, the latter is usually impossible). But don't try this unless the market is fairly lively, and you're not in a hurry...buyers are aware of this tactic, and it often helps other sensibly priced homes in the area sell quicker, making them look like great value! Read chapter 71 with advice on setting your price.

71

What is the right price?

When considering the value of your property, don't lose sight of the fact that normal rules of pricing apply to this marketplace. For example, £399,950 is a better listing price than £405,000. Why? Because we all prefer to buy goods under the hundred pound (or hundred thousand pound) bracket i.e. £99 rather than £100, and because, at £405,000, a buyer is just as likely to offer £395,000.

If you price your property at £399,950, and a buyer offers only £395,000, you can reply that you were told the property was worth £400,000 and that you only put it on the market at that price for a quick sale, no negotiating. In other words, you are more likely to achieve £399,950. The same applies for pricing at £899,950 in preference to £905,000, and so on. It's just human nature to be drawn to the figure in the lower price bracket.

In a sellers' market, you may wish to list your property with a *starting price* of £399,950 (or just under the price bracket relevant to your home). This could be advertised as 'Offers over £399,950 considered'. Of course, it doesn't mean all offers received will be above this price, but it does indicate to purchasers that offers below this price may not be considered.

Some further tips for determining the price:

- Do not add an agent's fees on top of your asking price. You may just be pricing yourself out of the market.

- Don't forget the basics of a saleable property:
  - The right home
  - At the right price
  - In the right market
  - For sale with an active and appropriate marketing strategy
- If you're serious about selling, forget about 'hope value'. Make sure the property is priced to sell. There is little chance a buyer will miraculously appear and want to pay you substantially more than market value. Consider this: if you expect someone to pay more than all the agents and research you've done suggests you'll receive, will *you* then pay over market value for someone else's home? I didn't think so.
- Check out your competition. That is, see what's for sale in direct competition with your property. What's listed locally at the same asking price you hope to achieve? How does your property rate compared to those similar properties purchasers will be viewing over the same weekend? Do they make your home look expensive or good value? Are they on a better or worse street? A large garden will be worth considerably more than a courtyard. As will a property decorated in 2010 compared with another which hasn't seen a lick of paint since 1975. A home in a popular school catchment area and within walking distance of facilities will be worth significantly more than one that isn't. You get the idea.
- Remember that every area has a ceiling price. That is, the maximum amount a buyer will spend on a property before they start to look elsewhere in a more prestigious street or area. If your home is

already at the top of the market for properties similar to yours in the area, don't get carried away with doing renovations - people just won't spend over a certain amount if they feel they can get more value (or kudos) from moving to the postcode next door.

Is your house the nicest for sale on the street?

Or the biggest? Or with the best price tag?

Which will sell first? Be honest and realistic...

- You could take the following mathematical approach as a guide for determining the right price, depending on your circumstances.

  1. Take the average price of three agents' valuations.
     e.g. Agent A values it at £700,000
           Agent B values it at £600,000
           Agent C values it at £620,000
     Average valuation = £640,000

  2. If you have All the Time in the World, list the property on the market at 10% more than the average valuation.
     e.g. £640,000 x 10% = £704,000

  3. If you have a Reasonable Time to Sell your property, list it at 5% more than the average valuation.
     e.g. £640,000 x 5% = £672,000

  4. If you are In a Rush, and don't want to lose out on a fantastic bargain currently for sale, list it at 3% below the average valuation.
     e.g. £640,000 x -3% = £620,800

- Set your asking price just above what you expect to achieve, especially as buyers often offer just below the asking price.

- Remember, it's not the final selling price that matters most, but the differential between the level you are selling, and the level at which you are buying. See Chapters 8–9.

72

Agents' commissions

Selling your property is not about what commission an agent charges. At the end of the day, it's about how much you get for your home, after the agents' fees.

Agents' fees can seem expensive, but do you really want to instruct the cheapest agent in the area? You get what you pay for, and a low-fee agent may well impact on the price you end up with. Think of it this way:

- How much effort do you think an agent will put into the sale of your property if they're only earning 1 per cent?
- How much can they afford to spend on advertising?
- How motivated will their negotiators be?

A good agents' commission level will generally be in the range of 2–3 per cent, depending on factors such as the state of the market, the area and the price of the property.

As will be discussed, if you go with multiple agents, it sets up a bit of competition. What you really want is two or three agents competing at full commission, all of them highly motivated to sell your property.

It is also well worth negotiating with your agent over the fee they charge. If your agent can achieve a price substantially over the asking price, perhaps you can offer an enhanced fee. If they get well below the value, and you only accept due to personal time constraints, then perhaps you can pay them a smaller fee.

Also, if your house is expensive, an agent might not flinch if you suggest 2 per cent instead of the normal 3 per cent.

Conversely, if you know it is a buyers' market, consider offering the incentive of a higher commission if the agent can land you a sale within 5 per cent of your asking price.

Not all estate agents will be prepared to negotiate. But it doesn't hurt to try, and in my experience most agents – around six out of 10 on average – will come down, depending, of course, on market conditions at the time.

Another way in which you can work with commission is to use the fee as a strategy. For instance, you might inform Agent A that, although he is charging 2.5 per cent, compared to the 2 percent charged by Agent B down the road, you are going to instruct him anyway. You like him, and you want him to do his best for you. And if he sells it, you'll pay his 2.5 per cent.

Would you step out onto the balcony for a moment?
Say you own a beautiful £300,000 flat and you need
to make a decent profit on the property to secure your
next home. You'd also like to sell the flat as quickly as
possible.

Agent A

- *Charges 2.5% commission.*
- *Appreciates your instruction and treats you as a switched-on vendor.*
- *Really motivated to sell your property as it's a good fee level.*
- *Gets asking price offer of £300,000.*
- *Cost of fees at 2.5%: £300,000 x 2.5% = £7,500.*
- *You walk away with: £300,000 — £7,500 = £292,500.*

Agent B

- *Cheapest agent in town and charges 1.75% commission.*
- *Little advertising for your property due to less money in the deal.*
- *Less viewings.*
- *Less motivated negotiators.*
- *Gets an offer of £290,000 (your flat really is lovely!!).*
- *Cost of fees at 1.75%: £290,000 x 1.75% = £5,075.*
- *You walk away with: £290,000 — £5,075 = £284,925.*

In this instance, with a motivated Agent A, charging a higher fee, you make an additional £7,575!

It's impossible to judge whether all agents charging lower commission levels are any better or worse than those who charge a higher fee. I'm sure there are plenty of cases where the lower charging agent achieves the price the vendor is after. It might just take a few weeks longer. In a sellers' market, it might not make a difference at all. It goes back to market conditions and which agent seems most trustworthy and knowledgeable, with a good track record for selling properties similar to yours in the area you live.

Finally, make sure that you add a covering letter to the standard Terms and Conditions (see Chapter 75), clarifying the commission terms or the sliding scale of commission you've agreed. Also make sure that the agent acknowledges this, by counter-signing the document, or by getting them to include the details within the Terms and Conditions.

73

Two agents are better than one

There are many decisions to make when selling your home. Do you sell privately? Do you use an estate agency? Do you use *multiple* estate agencies to increase your chances of a premium price? Which agents do you choose?

Once you find an agent you like, you will have to sign a listing agreement. This is like a contract, laying out the specifics of your arrangement, including how long you will let the agent represent your home and what the sales commission will be.

Many agents prefer you choose an exclusive listing, normally called 'a sole agency agreement'. My advice, upfront, is to avoid such an agreement. You may assume that, as an agent myself, I would recommend sole agency, and it's true, a vast majority of agents would suggest you take this route. One reason might be because it's a specialist property – such as a listed building – and they are experts in that field. However, the usual reason is, the likelihood of them selling your property is greatly increased if they're the only agent, so their chances of earning the commission are much higher.

Also, with a sole agency you may lose the right to sell your home privately.

Multiple agency arrangements are best, as they encourage competition. By choosing multiple agency you, as the seller, expose your property to the maximum number of potential buyers. Also, the more competition there is between the agents, the greater your chance of achieving the highest price.

In my opinion, sole agencies are a totally false economy. You save yourself less than 1 percent and create a lazy agent.

Agents respond best to competition. Agent A will work harder if he is aware that Agent B might sell your house first. Sometimes the buyer may be on Agent A and Agent B's books, ensuring both agents work not only harder, but faster.

Your ultimate goal is to get the best price for your property, not to pay the lowest commission.

Whatever you decide, commit for no longer than three months. In a good market, make that one month. If you find the agent lacking in enthusiasm, you won't want to be locked in.

74

Choosing the right agent

If you are a buyer, your choice will be about the right property. Fingers crossed that a good agent is selling it. However if you are a seller, the choice is yours, and you must choose with extreme care.

It's checklist time.

Firstly, you've found out as much as you can about prices for comparable types of property in the area, using the Internet, details in agents' windows, newspaper advertisements, and you've even had a surveyor around. Remember, knowledge is power!

You've done some mystery shopping.

- Do the negotiators seem friendly, approachable, and presentable?
- Do they specialise in particular types of property? (Some sell mostly flats, some concentrate on historic or top-of-the-market properties.)
- Is the office well located, and do they seem organised and in control as a team?
- Do they appear to be talking sense about values?

You've invited at least three agents, preferably five, for a valuation. Ideally, one of them should be from outside the immediate vicinity to get a more balanced view.

- Did they arrive on time?
- Do they look professional?
- Are they members of the necessary trade associations?
- Are they knowledgeable about the area and market trends?
- Do they have examples of marketing campaigns for similar properties to yours, as well as recent sales information to show you?
- How long is it taking them to sell well-priced homes at present?
- Can they suggest ways to increase the value of your home?
- Do they know how to negotiate (even if it's for their own fee!)?
- Have they provided a list of recent vendors for you to speak to? If not, can they?
- Do they appear interested in your home, and importantly, do you like them?
- What have they valued your home at? Can they qualify their valuation? What evidence do they have to support this value as being realistic?
- What are their charges?

Now here come the agents, one by one. Imagine handing each of them £10,000 of your own, hard-earned money. Which of them would you entrust it with the most? Remember, how long would it take you to earn £10,000 after tax? Please work out the answer – it's not a trick question.

After each agent has given you their valuation, decide which two you would depend on the most. They will not necessarily be the ones who gave you the highest valuation. Nor should it be the most amenable. Friendly is good. Soft is not.

75

Agency terms and conditions

Once you've decided on the agency you're going to use, contact them again and ask to speak to the person who valued your property by name. Tell him or her why you have chosen them – not only will they be flattered, but they will work harder to satisfy a discerning client – and that you'd like them to handle the sale of your home.

This constitutes an 'instruction to sell', and even if you don't get around to formally signing any written contract, this is considered legally binding. In general, though, your agent will now confirm their fees and other details in writing – their terms and conditions. Here are some of the more important aspects to watch out for:

Commission level

The agent's commission will generally be in the range of 2–3 per cent, depending on factors such as the state of the market, the area and the price of the property.

Other costs

Some agents may try to charge extra for brochures or print advertisements. Unless you're in the million pound plus market, you shouldn't need a higher level of publicity, or have a need to pay for this.

Length of contract

Be wary of entering into long contracts with any one agent, and be extra wary of long notice periods buried in the small print.

Often agents will agree to a four-week sole agency period, but have an eight-week notice period if you want to break, hidden somewhere in the small print.

If you are really determined to give someone a sole agency, then only offer it to them for two to three weeks. Write a letter to this effect on day one, stating the exact period of sole agency. Make it clear that you intend to review the agreement after the agreed period is up. Ideally, if you plan on instructing Agent B, the notice period for Sole-Agent A should run concurrently with the agreed agency period.

As mentioned previously, commit for no longer than three months (and, in a good market, make that one).

When discussing the listing agreement, talk through other issues, too. For instance, let the agent know if there are certain times when you want the house off-limits for viewings.

Sole selling rights

Reject any contract with these words in them. It means that, even if you sell the house to a friend or relative, the agent can still claim commission!

Everything should be made abundantly clear to you before you embark on any kind of contract. If you're not sure, just write 'no sale, no fee' on the document before you sign it.

76

Home truths

You stand a much better chance of selling your property if you have acknowledged any problems and reflected them in your asking price. If you've followed my advice and had a surveyor around to view the property, be upfront with agents and buyers as to any faults they've outlined.

By acknowledging a property's weaknesses openly, should a problem surface later on during the selling process, it's harder for a buyer to use this information as a means of reducing their offer.

I would also recommend that you ask your agent to tell you the worst thing about your home that may, in his or her opinion, affect its sale. This may be hurtful – perhaps you spent hours painting the hallway dark purple – but at least it gives you the chance to remedy the situation.

77

Marketing your home

Don't get lured into instructing an agency just because they've got a trendy looking bar as an office, or a flash advertisement in a national newspaper. An old-school marketing approach, even if it's wrapped up in fancy modern packaging, no longer provides the same results when it comes to producing viewings and buyers.

Today, the Internet is more important than ever when selling a property. An agent can be successful with only three tools: a good online marketing strategy, a telephone and a camera. Sure there are other strategies and techniques that can assist – but with a few brain cells and these three tools as essentials, the job's half done.

By 2007, 83 per cent of buyers were starting their search for UK property online…that's huge! Today, this figure would be even higher, especially taking into consideration the web-savvy, time-poor Londoner…

Internet advertising is key. You want an agent who will advertise your home (and themselves) on every possible online property portal with a focus and success rate in your area.

From Rightmove, to Zoopla and Findaproperty and the latest property search engines such as Globrix, check the portals and make sure your property is easily found. If not, hassle your agent until this is resolved.

One important site that cannot be overlooked is Google. Everyone searches on Google, and your agent should be trying their hardest to have fantastic search engine ranking. Do they use pay per click advertising (PPC)? Why don't you ask them?

In fact, visit Google and search for anything to do with property or apartments in your area. Who appears high in the ranking? These are the agencies your buyers are going to visit first when they begin their hunt for a home. If your property is not listed with them, how will they find out about your home?

Obviously, the Internet is always evolving and changing, and an agent's online ranking can alter – but it's important you instruct an agency who will work very hard to give your property every opportunity to be seen.

78

Why you should have a sales board

I can hear you already – you don't want a board! You don't want your neighbours to know your house is for sale. To be honest, it's really frustrating when people say this. My response is usually, 'Great, let's see just how long it will take us to sell this property!'.

Some people object to a board because they think it's just a free advertisement for the agent. Sure it is, but it's an even better advertisement for your home. Something like a quarter of all property sales are achieved thanks to a 'For Sale' board.

- A board is an advert 24 hours a day, seven days a week for your house.
- It keeps buyers on their toes, knowing that other people are aware that the house is For Sale.
- It shows you're serious about selling your house.
- When combined with Internet advertising, it eliminates time-wasters. If somebody sees your board, before they've even seen the inside of the house or know the price, they are familiar with where it's located, what the outside is like, how big it is, and can then research further details online if they like it. The same works in reverse: that is, potential buyers researching online can drive by and decide whether they like the look and feel of your home before arranging a viewing.
- It alerts anyone who wants to live in your street.

Yes, it might also encourage a few people knocking on your door asking to look around, but that is easy enough to deal with. Simply have some of the agent's cards to hand and tell them to make an appointment. This small inconvenience far outweighs the added interest the board will create.

Some council boroughs have restrictions on boards, especially in conservation areas, but if there is no legal reason stopping you, and you genuinely want to sell your home, then say yes to a board.

79

Energy Performance Certificates

(and a quick goodbye to HIPS)

Since May 2010, Home Information Packs (HIPS) have no longer been required to sell a home. One useful component from within the pack, the Energy Performance Certificate (EPC) has remained a legal requirement.

To comply with the new law, you need to have instructed a Domestic Energy Assessor (DEA) before marketing your home for sale. Whilst it is your responsibility as the seller to arrange and pay for the EPC, both yourself and your estate agent must make reasonable efforts to secure the completed EPC within 28 days.

Something to consider if you think you may be selling your property at any time in the future, is to have an EPC prepared in advance. An EPC is valid for 10 years at present, so there's no reason not to. One advantage is that you may find out you can very cheaply improve the energy efficiency of your home as part of your preparation for selling. This would not only improve your home's EPC rating and provide an immediate reduction in your fuel bills, but it could also increase the value of your property.

If you do make changes to your home, suggested in the EPC, most DEAs will update it and issue a new one for a small additional fee.

You can find a local DEA easily by:
- searching online using any search engine
- using the Government site: www.hcrregister.com

80 Learn the lingo

So, you've instructed the best local agents to market your property and they've come up with a suitable marketing strategy. Now it's time to learn the lingo!

The 'particulars', a rather Dickensian term I think, are the written details describing a property and provided by the estate agent to potential buyers.

Particulars Rule # 1: The best agent isn't always the one with the glossiest particulars.

Particulars Rule # 2: The language of the particulars does not make any difference. People don't go to view properties on the basis of fancy language. If you're not fooled, why should they be?

So why are properties described in such over-the-top terms?

Often it's just to keep the vendor happy. However, it's also true that estate agents were once renowned for their use of poetic licence in writing a property description. This all changed with the passing of the Property Misdescriptions Act 1991 which made it a criminal offence for the estate agent to wrongly describe a property offered for sale. Almost overnight, a thousand inappropriately flattering adjectives were consigned to the bin.

Despite this, agents have had decades of experience in hyping houses, so you should take what they say with a pinch of salt. Note also that the agents' particulars usually include a disclaimer.

Particulars Rule # 3: If a property is listed for sale through multiple agents, compare what each say about the place. Agents all have idiosyncrasies. Don't believe me? Find a house you know that's currently for sale, write your own summary of it and then compare it against the agent's details. By learning the language, you can make sure your property is properly represented.

Particulars Rule # 4: Always remember that a vendor can tell an agent what to write, or suggest changes to the agent's particulars, as long as they are truthful.

When your agent does complete the particulars, make sure you see them and check them carefully:

- Have they missed any special characteristics?
- Does their description accurately reflect the character of your home?
- Do the photographs show the property at its best?

Particulars Rule # 5: If your agent's particulars are good, but not great, don't worry about this too much. It won't make that much of a difference. Yes, check to make sure the fundamentals are correct, but if this is the case, don't spend weeks going to and fro to get them perfect. Just let the agent get on with the job of selling your property.

We've all played the game of comparing particulars with the reality, so here are some of the classics of agent-speak.

Architecturally designed:	Really? There's not a property in the country that hasn't been architecturally designed.
Vacant possession:	Well, you're hardly going to move into it with another family living there, are you?
Reduced for a quick sale:	On the market for a long time, sellers now desperate.
Traditional:	Old and crumbling.
Individual:	Almost everybody hates it.
Cosy:	Cramped.
Bijou:	Even more cramped.
Full of character:	Full of problems.
Well presented:	Tarted up for the sale.
In need of modernisation:	On its last legs.
Mature garden:	Lawn was mown a year ago.
Neat garden:	Concrete back yard.
Spacious:	Will cost a fortune to heat.
Light and airy:	Cold and draughty.
Potential for extension:	You can't swing a cat without one.
Easy to manage:	Tiny.
Secluded:	Don't even think about being able to walk to the shops.
Full of potential:	You'll need a fat bank balance.

No doubt, by the end of your buying or selling process, you'll have a few more to add to the list.

Once you've agreed on the particulars, make sure you have copies to hand at all times, just in case a would-be purchaser arrives without a copy.

81 Floorplans and virtual tours

Are floorplans and virtual tours a necessary evil, or do they provide too much information?

Most people aren't experienced at reading floorplans, so you have to be careful. For instance, you might think it's a good idea to include a floorplan if you're advertising your property on the web. However, this might put some people off. They might misinterpret the floorplan (or part of it), and decide not to view the house. Too much information can be counter-productive.

As a seller, you want as many people as possible to view your property. As a buyer, you should be getting out and seeing as many homes as you can, not simply relying on floorplans to make your decision for you.

Similar arguments apply over virtual tours – i.e. 360 degree video tours – viewed on the web. Sure, they're great, and vendors are clamouring for them. But images don't tell the whole story. In fact, a virtual tour can make a property look much smaller than it actually is.

Potential buyers need to get a feel for the place, suss out the atmosphere, and rely on their gut instinct as to whether they like it.

I don't go for virtual tours. I don't want to satisfy the buyers' lust for technology. I want to get them in and evoke the memories of a fireplace similar to what they had when living with their parents as a child.

Floorplans and virtual tours only tell part of the story, and they're a pretty superficial way of seeing a property.

The best thing your agent can do for you is get on the telephone and encourage people to come round and see it for themselves.

Too much information over the web or in a set of details can work against you. The people who love the glossy stuff are the sort of people who have agreed to buy your home already and use the virtual tours and floorplans to show it off to their mates.

82

What buyers really want

So let's cut to the chase. What do buyers really want when searching for a new property – and what's going to help sell your home quicker?

Is it flavoured property descriptions? We all know they're taken with a grain of salt.

Floorplans? If a purchaser has spent a long time looking for a particular-sized property and remains open enough to compromise on layout (really, if buyers want to see a floorplan before viewing a property, you have to question whether it helps your cause).

Virtual tours? If their Internet connection is sophisticated enough to handle the large file size (and most certainly not whilst they're trying to sneak a quick look at work during their lunch break).

Podcasts? Hello? No thanks. Just a fancy marketing spin for an agent to win your instruction.

Have you guessed what buyers really want? It's photographs. And the more the better.

Think about your searching process. It's the photograph in the advertisement that gets your attention, whether it's online or flicking through a newspaper. The better the photos, the more effective the advertisement will be, and the more calls and emails you'll receive to view your property.

Photographs are one of the most important tools when selling your property. This means it's up to you to ensure:

1. Your home is sparkling for the photographer:

   - All bench tops to be clear of clutter (including kitchen, bathroom, coffee and bedside tables).
   - Dishes to be washed and put away and tea towels removed from view.
   - Magnets to be taken off the fridge.
   - All cupboard doors closed (you'd think I wouldn't have to mention this…).
   - Blinds, curtains and adjoining doors to other rooms open for best light.
   - Beds to be made.
   - Toys cleared away.
   - Toilet seats down.
   - Lawns mowed and the garden tidied up.

2. The agent or the photographer (good agents these days will arrange a professional to take the shots) should take *lots* of photos of your property – at every angle. If you have any special features or a great view, make sure these are captured.

   Through various studies Rightmove.co.uk have conducted on behalf of their agents, they inform us that an average property listed on their website, with more than one photo, will have a click-through rate for further information 115 per cent higher than a property *without* a photo.

   There are many examples of properties being listed for months, marketed with an average, dreary looking exterior photograph as the main image. Then after a few months, when the agent finally realises the photos aren't showing the home in the best light, they change the main image to that of the beautiful view from the bedroom, or the cosy reception with a fire burning.

Guess what happens? They sell the home in days, after being listed for weeks without a single enquiry. A coincidence? I think not.

3. If you're not satisfied with the photographs taken, and they don't show your home in its best light, do something about it. Remember, the photographers are not miracle workers and, at the end of the day, you provided the canvas. Also remember that it's not their job to tidy your home on arrival. But if, for genuine reasons, important shots were missed, or they chopped off half the room in the image, ask the agent for the photos to be retaken. Or, you can supply the photos yourself if you're unsatisfied.

83

First impressions count

We call it 'kerb appeal'. Your house should make a good first impression, even from the street. Buyers often drive past a property for sale, and if they don't like the look of it at first glance, they'll strike it off their list. So don't underestimate the importance of first impressions.

Yes, there will be some things you can't do anything about (such as electricity pylons or a neighbour's unkempt lawn), but at least make sure you maximise your chance of a sale by sprucing up your own patch.

I like to compare it to walking into a dimly lit discount retail store. The clothes rails are unorganised with garments lying all over the floor, you can't find what you're after without digging through unorganised piles, and the place could do with a good scrub. Have you got this image in your mind? Now compare it to the retail shop across the road, brightly lit, clothes in an orderly fashion and arranged by colour and size…ah, bliss. This doesn't mean that you wouldn't buy from the first disorderly store – it will, however, impact on the *price* you're willing to pay for their goods. The same principle can be applied to your home (remember that £10,000 I mentioned earlier?).

Step over to the other side of your street and take a long, hard look at your house. What does it look like from here? How does it compare to the neighbours'?

Walk towards the front door, noting what could do with attention. For instance:

- Make sure the drive or pathway is clear of toys, bikes, prams, roller blades and so on.
- Could the fences or garden walls be tidied up without too much effort?
- If there's a garden gate, make sure it's oiled and works smoothly.
- Weed the flower beds, prune the trees and shrubs, and mow the lawn.
- Think about adding some tubs of flowers, hanging baskets or other colourful foliage.
- Paint the front door if needed.
- Polish up the letterbox, house number and other accessories.
- Make sure the doorbell works.
- Clear up garden hoses and tools.
- Do the same for the back garden, making sure rubbish bins and other eyesores are tidied away.

Now go up on the balcony and be completely objective and unemotional. Ask yourself the question, 'What would an average buyer like?' For instance, you may be partial to garden gnomes, but you may well be in the minority. None of this, 'Well they just have to accept my house as it is' attitude.

Now step back and reassess your kerb appeal.

84 Clear the clutter and clean

If your home is a tip, no amount of smooth talking from an agent taking people around is going to help sell it. I'm glad to say that it is not our job to clean up after you, or to rearrange the lighting to show off your home to its best advantage. That's your job, and you should take it seriously.

In my time I've shown clients around properties that were frankly embarrassing, with adult toys lying around the bedroom and evidence of crazy parties from the night before. Some homes look like a pigsty…who wants to buy a house from a pig? Teenager's bedrooms are one of the worst potential disaster areas. If necessary, bribe your teens to keep them tidy during the viewing period!

Even a note to the cleanest, tidiest family in town, the reality is that you are probably going to need to do at least a few things to spruce up your home. The most effective action of all is to clear away the clutter.

Make some space, move unnecessary furniture into the attic, basement or garage. Better still, get it off the property altogether. Self-storage depots are an invaluable tool for the house mover. They're inexpensive and convenient, and you can temporarily store all the junk you don't want to throw out.

Try:

www.store-safe.co.uk
www.storing.com
www.self-store.co.uk
www.safestore.co.uk
www.thebigyellow.co.uk

Once the main clutter is out of the way:

- Clean stains from kitchen sinks, bathrooms and toilets.
- Clear post and junk mail from the communal hallway.
- Get your carpets professionally cleaned.
- Put in brighter light bulbs.
- Remove net curtains and clean your windows.
- Tidy away knick-knacks, bottles and cosmetics.

Think about the overall package you're presenting. If it's not your thing, there are many home staging companies and house doctors out there who are willing to offer a free initial consultation to discuss your home's potential, and, of course, the value of their services.

The London-based company we recommend to our clients offer a free half-hour consultation. Their services have helped many of our vendors sell their home in either:

- a quicker time frame; or
- for more money than otherwise possible.

A recent example resulted in four offers and the home sold to the highest bidder, within a week!

Believe me, these seemingly insignificant details can add many thousands of pounds to your eventual sale price.

85

Clear the air

Apart from clearing the clutter and giving your home a good scrub, there are plenty of other ways you can spruce up the place to make it look and feel desirable.

Don't be tempted to spend big money on your home before selling it. You paint a wall green, and a buyer will paint it blue. Instead, concentrate more on odours, lighting, ventilation and warmth.

Most importantly, have you thought about how your house smells? Ask a friend to be brutally honest. Stale cigarette smoke is one of the worst offenders.

If you've got pets, you probably don't even notice that your house smells of them, or that their hair is everywhere – but the buyer will. I once went to view a house where the owner was boiling up bones for his dogs. It smelt revolting and I couldn't look around the rooms without gagging. I guess he didn't really want to sell it after all.

It's an old cliché that the smell of freshly baked bread or real coffee brewing will give a house a 'homely' aroma that will appeal to buyers. Okay, not many of us have got the time to bake bread (or know how to), but at least we can make sure the place smells nice. Before a viewing, open the windows and air the whole house. Fresh flowers also help, and make the place seem cared for. Scented candles are another option.

If you're trying to sell an empty house, leave the heating on low and get some furniture in to make the place look a bit more habitable.

86

Appointments to view

There are two schools of thought as to how many appointments an agent should make to show intending buyers around your house. The first is that a good agent will only send around three or four quality buyers, on the basis that he knows his buyers and thus saves everybody a lot of time. The second is that the more people who see a property, the higher the chance of selling it. Buyers are always changing their requirements, and once they've seen your house they might decide that they're interested, even if it doesn't exactly fit their previous criteria.

I go along with the second approach. It may not be ideal in the sense that sometimes the agent will be showing people around who aren't really interested, but don't let this bother you. As a vendor, you want to make sure that as many people as possible see your home.

A third way of dealing with appointments is to arrange a show day, or open house. Originally an American idea, it was first used in the UK for showcasing luxury flats, but is now used for all types of properties. Show days are usually conducted over the weekend for an hour or so, with the agent overseeing viewings, but letting potential buyers stroll through at their leisure.

Once again, the more people who view (and see others viewing), the better. Also, people feel under less pressure on a show day, so generally more of them come. Make sure your agent has the name and contact details of everyone that enters your property (for follow-up and security). It may be wise to lock away any valuables on the day.

Make sure the washing up's done, the beds are made and there's no mess lying around. Ensure there is adequate light by opening the curtains, and turn on bedside lamps to brighten up the bedrooms. Make the property cosy and inviting.

This may prove to be a good option for you if you're busy or have small children. It means you can get a lot of buyers through your home in one day (and one clean-up!). It is best if you pop out for a coffee whilst the open house takes place. Just leave the agent to do his job. Buyers are more at ease without the owners peering around the kitchen cupboards listening for feedback. The agent should give you an update at the end of the day and also a few days later with any offers that have come out of the inspection.

Even if you're not having a show day, it's fine for two people to view your property at once as it creates competition. You might have to apologise in advance for any mix up in the arrangements.

Finally, if you are going to give the instructed agents keys to your home, get enough sets cut for each agency. It is concerning to think that the two best agencies in town, that you've instructed to sell your most important possession, will be squabbling amongst themselves as to who had the set of keys last, or who has the most applicants going to view that morning, therefore needing the keys – but they will (it's all part of the competition of multiple agency). Or even worse, you may find a negotiator can't be bothered to go down the road to the other agency to collect your keys because they don't like walking into their competitor's office, or they think it's too cold, showing their applicant something else (for which they do have the keys) instead.

87

Viewings and security

It doesn't happen very often, but unscrupulous people can use a house viewing as an opportunity to steal small items, or to check out the place for a subsequent burglary.

In terms of your general security and safety, if you're selling privately, never show anyone around without first getting their name and telephone number, and then calling them back to check that they are bona fide. At least you'll have a name and number for everybody who visits the house for your own record keeping.

If in doubt, don't show.

It goes without saying that no vendor, male or female, should ever allow a stranger to enter their house unannounced purely on the basis that they have spotted a 'For Sale' board outside. Refer them back to the agents.

To save you any worry, make sure you put valuables or jewellery away throughout the whole selling period. That way you don't have to think about it when people come to view.

Additionally, you might want to check with your insurance company to make sure you're covered if your agent has a key, and when he or she is showing people around your home.

It may also be worth asking the question of your agents as to the security measures they have in place to protect the anonymity of your keys whilst kept in their office. You'll find that *most* agents have a fairly secure key system in place.

88 How best to show your property

You've got two choices when it comes to showing people around: either do it yourself or leave it to the agent. Generally, I recommend the latter. We have more experience than you, are less emotionally involved, and we know when, in the viewing process, to keep our mouths shut. In any case, if the homeowner is working during the day it is much easier to let the agent have the keys and get on with it.

Sometimes, though, you will want to show viewers around yourself. Perhaps the agent has booked a second viewing after office hours, or at the weekend. If so, here are a few tips to make sure it all goes smoothly:

- Always show your house in a clockwise direction. Decide which is the best room in your house and start at the opposite end (or downstairs), going around clockwise, before, if applicable, going upstairs. You would be amazed at how many people forget to show a room.
- Children and animals can be a major distraction. Send the kids outside to play or confine them to one room so they're not underfoot the whole time. Keep pets well out of the way (especially over-friendly and bouncy dogs). Get someone to take the dog for a walk if necessary.

- Do a last-minute vacuum, clean up the kitchen, make the beds, tidy up, light a fire if you have one, and light some scented candles 30 minutes or so before the viewers arrive.
- Please, make sure all loo seats are down.
- Try not to blabber or to state the obvious ('this is the bathroom'). Point out your home's good features, but try not to oversell. Give viewers a copy of the particulars if they don't have them, so they can make notes.
- Be chatty and friendly, but also give people the chance to roam and take their time without feeling crowded or pressured. Give them the space to imagine living in your house.
- Don't feel that you have to show every single power point and feature. Remember, often on a first appointment people just want to get an idea of what the house is like. Heavy selling will just turn them away.
- At the end of the viewing, ask them if there's anything else they want to know. This gives them a chance to ask about local services, transport, and the neighbourhood vibe.
- On a second appointment, always let people wander around by themselves. Explain at the start that you're sure they would prefer to look around and chat alone rather than have you trailing them. It makes them feel less pressured.
- Finally, neither you nor your agent can sell your home to someone who doesn't want to buy it. Know when to give up.

89 Staying in control

Make sure you stay in control of the process by keeping a diary of detailed notes on all discussions. Most importantly, keep a diary of everyone who has viewed, and which agent they came through. This can save a lot of arguments later between agents if there is any kind of dispute about who the buyer came through. If this kind of dispute does arise, do not exchange contracts. Tell both agents and the buyer to sort it out between themselves. Don't kid yourself, if the matter is not resolved, and you go ahead and exchange, you could be liable for two sets of fees.

After you've had a few viewings, ask each estate agent:

- What did the viewers think of the house?
- Is there anything major they criticised that could be put right?
- If appointments were broken, why?
- Was the property hard to find? Are clearer directions needed?

Meanwhile, keep a written record of the following information from each agent:

- How many times has the property been advertised in the press?
- How easy is the property to find on the property portals online?
- When is it next being advertised or featured?

- How many viewing appointments have been made this week?
- How many can you expect next week?

Always ask your agent how the property market is behaving in general, and how this might affect potential buyers.

If no (or only very low) offers have come in after a few weeks on the market, talk to your agents about reviewing the price but, remember, work with, not against them.

90

How to respond to an offer

When an offer comes in, step straight out onto your balcony and ask:

Why is the buyer offering this price?
Is it all they can afford, or are they following advice?
Is this all they think it's worth? What if they're right?

Has the agent told them to start at that level?

Let's deal with this in two parts:

Firstly, let's imagine the agent has come back to you with an offer which is not entirely to your dislike. Whatever you do, don't say, 'Thank you very much, that is much better than I thought!'

The position of the buyer is just as important as the amount of the offer. For example, if you accept the offer too readily, the other parties might wonder if they could have got it cheaper (and might therefore use that hunch to come back later with a lower offer). It does happen.

And, remember, all offers are meaningless until you are sure the buyers can proceed. What if they are hoping for a 100 per cent mortgage and have County Court judgments against them? In that case, they're not much use to you as a purchaser.

Your best response to any offer below the asking price is,

'That sounds encouraging, but before I respond formally I just need to check with my partner/husband/wife/solicitor/son/daughter/friend for their views. However, I do think the purchaser will have to offer more [unless of course they have offered the full price]. *What do you think they will go up to?'*

Then be silent for as long as you have to, until the agent responds. Then comment:

'I'm not really 100 per cent sure, I will come back to you.'

Any questions where an agent or buyer asks, 'What price will you take?' are absolutely fine. Just respond with,

'I am unsure at this moment in time what my best option is, which is why I want to think about it.'

However, add:

'Do you think the purchaser will offer any higher?'

Before responding formally to the offer, allow a few hours or even a day to pass.

Your next response should be along the lines of:

'It's almost there. My wife/brother/sister/solicitor thinks I should accept it, but it is a little lower than I wanted. Please see if they will increase.'

I understand that some people feel uncomfortable trying to push the price up that little bit extra, but do remember what we said about earning that extra £10,000. Keep focused on that goal!

91 Know your buyer

Whatever the offer, you must be sure the buyer is really in a position to do the deal. This is your opportunity to reciprocate the overload of questions you received from the buyer (or at least you would have received, had they read this book!).

The questions you need to ask (you may feel more comfortable with the agent asking them on your behalf), include:

- Does the buyer have anything to sell?
- If they claim to be first-time buyers, get clarity on this.
- If their property is for sale, how long has it been on the market?
- If their property is under offer, what is the position of *their* buyer? Do they have anything to sell?
- What are the buyer's mortgage arrangements?
- How much are they borrowing? And how realistic is it that the mortgage will be approved?
- How long do they want for exchange?
- How long for completion?
- Are they expecting anything to be left in the property?'

You must be sure of your buyer's motives. Dig into their reasons for buying – for instance, it may be because they have a job pending (what if they don't get the job?), or maybe that they have chosen to live in your area without having researched it properly (what if they change their mind?). Once you have done a little digging, grade the applicants between one and five.

To help in your grading, there is no reason why you can't get your mortgage broker to speak to theirs. This should really satisfy any question of whether they are in a position to proceed.

Don't rush in and accept an offer purely because you're desperate for a sale. If you are happy with an offer, but the prospective purchasers have their own property to sell first, explain to them that, price-wise, it is fine, but you don't want them wasting money on a survey if they aren't yet in a position to proceed. If they are in a chain (waiting for their sale to complete before they can buy your property) and desperate to have the offer agreed, they could think about taking out a bridging loan (which can be a very expensive way to borrow money), or come back to you once they can proceed. Their need (or want) of having a property agreed and waiting, is not a reason for you to accept an offer from an unsuitable buyer.

I repeat, do not put any sale in hand until your buyer has an offer on their house from an unencumbered purchaser.

Another approach is that, legally, you can accept an offer, but keep your property on the market, especially if you're worried the potential buyer might not sell their own property for a long time. If they are your only hope, you could offer to pay back their abortive costs if you end up selling it elsewhere prior to them getting an acceptable offer on their property. However, tell the buyer that this is your intention on day one.

Also, to tie up your sale, encourage the buyer to enter into a Goodwill Charter or equivalent, drawn up by the solicitors (see Chapter 15).

92

Reasons to hold out for the right price

In order to get the price you want, you need to negotiate from your balcony. You need to use facts, not emotions. Throwing your toys out of the pram because things aren't going your way won't help anyone.

So how do you get the buyers to increase their offer? As I said, stick to the facts.

Inform the agent that the offer is not good enough, because, for instance:

- The house down the road sold for £x and you have spent an additional £y on yours.
- Your house is bigger, or is in better condition, or has a larger garden, or an extra bedroom than the one down the road.

Or:

- Your house has only been on the market for x weeks. You have had valuations from two other agents, both higher than the offer in question. Therefore you would like to give it more time.

Or:

- You don't dispute that the offer is realistic, but in order for you to be able to buy the house that you want, you need to achieve the asking price.

As with all aspects of the buying and selling process, if your gut instinct tells you to accept the offer, don't hold out just for the sake of it, or to avoid losing face. You may be better off accepting a slightly lower offer and moving on with your life than paying another six months mortgage payments, only to end up accepting the same offer later down the line (after you've missed out on your dream property and caused some pretty major strain on your relationship).

Other important considerations, apart from the price offered, include:

- How much deposit are they offering? Will this be cash?
- What are the buyer's terms and conditions, including time frames for exchange and completion?
- Are there any contingency clauses that weaken their offer?

I've talked elsewhere in the book about holding out for that extra £10,000, and I've talked now about trying not to be too brave.

How do you, as a vendor, know which road to take?

The answer is 48 hours. It's very unlikely you'll be able to play the game after this amount of time. Especially if you *have* to sell.

93

The agent's view

You might think that it's in your agent's interest to get the highest possible price for your property, but look at it this way…Imagine that you have received an offer of £690,000 on your £700,000 home. This offer may be close to the asking price, but it's still £10,000 less in your pocket. This is a large sum of money, and everything you have read so far in this book urges you not to overlook the importance of sums of this magnitude.

But what does your agent's firm think about this, and whose interest are they *really* considering? Let's take into account the firm's point of view. If the agency's commission on the sale is set at 2.5 per cent, and the sale goes through at £690,000, they will earn £17,250. A nice commission cheque, yes.

If you suggest that you want to hold out for the full asking price of £700,000, because you want (and should be able to achieve) the extra £10,000, as far as they're concerned, this means a rise in commission of only a further £230.

2.5% x £690,000 = £17,270

2.5% x £700,000 = £17,500

Let's take it a step further and consider the negotiator, working hard on your sale. He or she earns say, 15 per cent commission on the overall 2.5 per cent earned by the agency. So, with an offer in at £690,000, he stands to earn £2,587.

Working a whole extra two days to achieve your extra £10,000 earns him only £37.50 more.

In other words, is it really worth the agent's efforts in trying to achieve an offer with an extra £10,000?

Thus, there is an inbuilt tension between what you want and what your agent wants.

There is, of course, a win-win scenario. Why not, on instruction, offer to pay 1.5–2 per cent commission on any accepted offer up to £690,000 and then 20 per cent commission on anything above this. This focuses the negotiator and the agency to get you an above asking price offer, you get closer to your additional £10,000 and, hey presto, everyone's happy.

Now get back on the balcony. What would you do in your agent's shoes? He has 20 more appointments lined up and is clearly very busy with other properties. Is it his main priority to chase an extra £10,000 on your home when there's only £37.50 in it for him? The view from the balcony says that maybe the vendor needs to play a little hardball, and throw the whole negotiation back to the agent to come up with more money (either through negotiating a sliding scale commission early on, or perhaps offering a bonus if the negotiator achieves the extra £10,000 on the offer). There may be a few more pips to be squeezed out of this lemon yet.

94

Be prepared to switch agents

Selling a property can be a frustrating, stressful experience. I beg you to stay cool during the process.

- Don't build up your hopes.
- Be calm and unemotional.
- Be cynical (that doesn't mean dishonest).

Just because the process might seem to have ground to a halt does not mean you should become passive. Sit down with your agent and discuss the problems. It can be only one of three things:

- The price.
- The presentation.
- Marketing.

Usually, price is the culprit, which can lead to negative feedback from buyers and unmotivated selling agents. It is often the case that the property on an estate agent's books for the longest period usually ends up being sold by a new negotiator to the firm. Why? They have no knowledge of any negative history surrounding the property. They can look at the property with fresh eyes and sell it accordingly.

If after, say, two months your agents haven't sold your property, you are sure that you haven't overpriced it, and you've sat down with them to discuss the situation with no real positive outcome, then I recommend you change agents.

95

When all else fails...

Every property is saleable. Most problems with hard-to-sell properties are ultimately curable.

If we analyse 10 sales that have fallen through, probably only three of those concern a problem with the property itself. The other seven will have failed for reasons to do with the buyers and sellers. Those three unsold houses will still get sold, eventually.

Here's what you should do when your sale or purchase hits troubled waters and looks like it's going to fall through:

- Write down exactly what the issue is:
  - Is there another offer?
  - Has the surveyor or the solicitor encountered a problem?

Now go back to your Balcony Form and quantify in money terms how much it is going to cost if you still want to go ahead with this sale or purchase:

- How much will it cost to put right the problems my surveyor or solicitor has highlighted? (It's often the case with legal and structural problems that different professionals have substantially differing opinions on how much it will cost to fix something. So be prepared to get a second opinion and cost that into your calculation.)

- How much should I decrease/increase my offer by? Or, if you're the vendor, what is the minimum price you'll accept (with this new knowledge)?
  - When you have calculated the cost of correcting the problem, deduct from it all the fees you will have wasted if the sale is terminally aborted.
  - Add in your legal costs, survey costs, mortgage costs and any other costs you might incur if you started all over again, including allowances for time off work, extra rent or a bridging loan.
  - Take that net figure, add it to the price of the property, and see how it compares to the figure on your Balcony Form.

Imagine discussing the whole scenario with a third party. First, play the part of your opposite number, so that you really get to defend and understand their position. Then play the part of the third party observer, describing what he's seen.

Just stay commercial, not emotional, in the whole process.

Now move forward.

96 Deadlines

Setting deadlines can be interpreted as a sign of weakness, suggesting you're either desperate, or bluffing. In any case, solicitors, mortgage companies or surveyors simply ignore deadlines, leaving you with egg on your face. Better to explain to your solicitor at the start why you need a quick exchange, ask them what's a reasonable time period in your circumstances, and then enter into a Goodwill Charter or Lock-out Agreement (see Chapter 15).

You and your purchaser could, at the outset of a sale, agree a date that you would like to exchange contracts by, and tell all parties a date two weeks earlier (with only you and your buyer knowing about the leeway). Human nature dictates they will move the paperwork to the top of the pile.

If you have a sale in hand and feel the purchaser is dragging their feet or is no longer serious, put a deadline on it. However, be prepared to stick to it. Don't waiver. Better to draw the line and start looking for another purchaser than to keep hoping something positive will happen.

But do not set a deadline if you're simply trying to bluff your way out of a problem that's solvable. If allowed to proceed at their own pace, your buyer may well come around to accepting your offer or speeding up the transaction. Give them a tight deadline and they may well just walk away.

*One thing I've learnt about deadlines and
negotiation is that, if you pressure someone
who is only 50 per cent keen to proceed, once given
a deadline, they'll always pull out. So, look down
from your balcony, unemotionally, at why you wish
to issue a deadline. If it's only to reduce the period
of stress, be prepared to deal with a few more weeks
of misery – at least you will be able to get on with
your life eventually. But, if someone has been
messing you around, insisting they are about to
exchange, yet nothing happens, week after week,
you may have no choice but to set a deadline. If
that is the case, agree a date with the other party
and stick to it.*

If time is really tight, deadlines can be linked with incentives. Say a property is for sale at £400,000 and someone offers £390,000. The vendor could agree, but only if contracts are exchanged within 14 days. If they're not, the price returns to £400,000.

That'll bring everyone's concentration back to the table!

97

Conditional contracts

A conditional contract is a far more secure way of increasing the likelihood of your sale/purchase completing. Let me explain.

Take a buyer. Normally, when his solicitor tells him it's time to exchange, they have spent the last three to four weeks going through the searches and getting lots of questions answered. Perhaps if it's a flat, they've arranged the landlord's approval to sell the lease to them, or maybe they've been getting in an abundance of service charge history, so they know exactly what expenditure is coming up.

Now during that period, either party can change their mind, even with a Goodwill Charter or Lock-out Agreement. The best you can expect back is your bond – and hopefully the other party's. But sorry, no flat! So, if we rewind to earlier and all parties are ready to exchange, but the only thing holding it up is waiting for the searches to come in, or the mortgage offer, etc., exchange contracts on the condition that these outstanding issues will be satisfactorily solved.

Both parties are now locked in and can get on with the job of planning for the near future, safe in the knowledge that the deal is done and no-one can pull out, unless there is something dreadful in those searches.

I really buy into the concept of conditional contracts and think our whole conveyancing system should be built around them. People would not have to buy or sell if there was a real problem with the property, but they would be committed to the deal if they woke up one morning and decided that they no longer fancied going ahead with it.

Solicitors don't like conditional contracts. They argue that, if there are too many unresolved points in the contract, people still have the opportunity to wriggle out of them – therefore, there is not much point. But let's go back to my abortive rate of sales figure. If, in my opinion, only one in 10 agreed sales fall through for a real, genuine reason, surely any conditional contract is better than testing fate?

98 Remember the BATNA

As explained in Chapter 50, BATNA is an acronym for 'Best Alternative to a Negotiated Agreement'. In other words, what happens if this deal doesn't proceed? What are the *alternatives*? Is there an achievable outcome that ensures everybody wins?

In the BATNA, which forms part of the Balcony Form reproduced on page iv, you will see a number of questions that need to be raised, according to circumstances. The form should be addressed from the point of view of both the vendor and the purchaser, regardless of your position in reality.

The purpose of the BATNA is to encourage you to see both sides of the impasse, and to separate your feelings about the deal from the facts.

If you can really empathise with what both sides need, this could help you see a way forward, unblocking the process to everyone's advantage.

Doing a deal behind your agent's back

99

It's amazing how many people try it on, but may I warn you...do not do a deal behind your agent's back. It is fraudulent, it is illegal, and you are likely to be caught.

The relevant phrase in law is 'effective cause of introduction'. This means that, for example, if there's an agent's board outside your property and someone unknown to the agent knocks on the door and ends up buying your house, you are still liable to pay the agent their agreed commission. The agent can claim that the board was the 'effective cause'.

Because this is a recurring problem, agents make stringent checks as to who eventually buys the properties on their books. We also talk to each other so we know whether a property has been dealt with through the proper channels, or if someone is trying to pull a fast one.

The same applies if one buyer comes through an agent and then that same buyer, views your property for a second time, via another agent. Don't listen to the agent if he says 'That's fine, it's no problem, we do this all the time'. In most cases, if you sell through the second agent, you'll end up paying two sets of fees.

Don't contemplate trying the system if the opportunity presents itself. Agencies have so many systems for establishing who has seen your property and who ends up buying it, that it's not worth the headache, and on top of this, you can be prosecuted.

100 Selling without an agent

Around 5 per cent of all homes in Britain – or one in 20 – are sold privately. It's not something you would expect me to encourage, is it? Of course, the main reason people do it is to save on the agent's commission, but that commission is in return for a wide range of duties and responsibilities. I would not recommend selling your property privately, unless you are confident of your skills in the following areas:

- Local knowledge.
- Setting an achievable price.
- Preparing and producing the details, writing copy and taking photographs.
- Advertising the house.
- Maintaining a buyers' database.
- Arranging viewings (and remaining calm as buyers criticise your property).
- Negotiating the price.
- Dealing with offers and queries from the buyer.
- Finalising the sale.
- Legal protection.
- Being available for buyers' inspections.

Nor would I recommend selling privately unless your house is a very attractive proposition, set at a good price, and at a time when the market is reasonably active.

The view from the balcony here is quite clear. Someone is trying to save themselves 2 per cent on the most important investment they own, and they are totally losing sight of the real value, i.e. the price they end up getting for their property. Far too obsessed on saving pennies, this could end up costing them serious pounds.

Also remember that if you instruct an agency and sign their terms and conditions with 'no sale, no fee', there is nothing stopping you from trying to sell your property privately, at the same time! There is nothing to pay unless the property is sold to a purchaser introduced through the agency, for a price you're happy to sell for. You're in control. If you still decide to proceed on your own, there are a number of options. You will certainly need to decide where to advertise, for example on the Internet, in local papers, national papers or specialist property magazines.

Preparing private advertisements

If you are selling your property privately, you will need to pay particular attention to the wording of your advertisements. It is quite a skill to draw the reader's attention and get all the facts across in as short a space as possible.

Make sure you include the following basic information:
- The area (but not the street name).
- The type of property (e.g. flat, house or bungalow).
- If it's a flat, which floor is it on?
- Description of condition.
- Extra features, e.g. central heating, garage, garden.

- Full summary of accommodation, e.g. entrance hall, two bedrooms, reception, kitchen, bathroom.
- The overall square footage (see Chapter 11 to determine this).
- Price.
- Your phone number and/or email address.

Also, make sure you put 'no agents' on the advert, so that you don't get bothered by estate agents wanting to sell your home on your behalf.

In terms of advertising your property with photographs, this is essential. A picture really does tell a thousand words and can have a large impact on the response you receive to your advertising (whether online or in print). Make sure the image sells your home in its best light. I would recommend using a nice interior shot of a large reception or open-plan kitchen, or perhaps a photo of your garden or the fantastic view from your bedroom. If you have an attractive exterior shot, this will also work well. Contact the publication where you are advertising your private listing and check the quality and file size required for production. Try to advertise your property on as many private listing websites as possible; they offer a cheaper alternative to advertising in the press and, to top it off, you should be able to advertise as many photos of your property as you wish, all for the same price. See Chapter 61 for a list of sites you might wish to investigate.

Above all, I must remind you of the need to vet all applicants coming to view your property. See Chapter 87 for some of the precautions and insurance implications you will need to consider. For example, do not show anyone around until you have their name and phone number and you have called them back to confirm they are authentic. Also, never admit cold-callers without an appointment, or when you are alone in the property.

101 Congratulations, you've exchanged!

It's definitely time to pop that cork and celebrate. In fact, why don't you invite the buyers around for a drink? It's an exciting time for them also. This way, you can go through all the finer details of the house, such as where the important switches and knobs are hidden and which tap you use for the hose connection. Also, any last-minute hitches, such as your removal men not showing up on time, will be accepted in a much more gracious manner after this act of hospitality.

After a fun night of celebration there is a lot to be organised. With an upcoming move it is no surprise that important things are often overlooked. Use the checklist below a couple of weeks before to make sure you've got everything covered:

Change of address service: www.iammoving.com is a website that allows you to notify many of your service providers, including gas and telephone companies of your new address.

Have you contacted your local council? You'll need to contact your local council for a couple of reasons. First, get in touch with the council tax office to let them know the date you move out of your current property and when you move into your new one so they bill you correctly. Next, find the right person to speak to regarding removal permits and resident parking (for your new address), as these can take about two weeks to issue.

Have you redirected your post? You can download the form from the Post Office website. It can take up to 10 days to set up and there is a charge. See www.royalmail.com

Have you told the utility providers (gas, water, electricity)? You need to tell them at least 48 hours in advance that you are moving. Pass on the details of your current supplier to the people moving in. On your moving day you will need to read the meters in both properties so the correct bills can be issued. When you move into your new home, contact who you want to supply your utilities so they can register you as a new customer.

Have you arranged for your final telephone bill and a new connection at your new home? You may be able to transfer your existing number.

Have you informed your bank, building society, credit card and insurers? You may also need to alter or cancel direct debits you have for your old home.

Have you updated your driving licence? Visit the Driver and Vehicle Licensing Agency (DVLA) website to find out how: www.direct.gov.uk/en/Motoring/index.htm

Have you updated your details on the Electoral Register? The register is updated every month and you need to be included on it to vote. You can download the form from the Electoral Commission's website www.electoralcommission.org.uk/elections/voter-registration and then send it to your Electoral Registration Office, which is based at your local council.

Have you told TV Licensing? Your TV licence will need to be transferred. You can do this online (www.tv-l.co.uk).

Have you decided what you do and don't want to take? There are lots of charities that will gladly have your unwanted items, including charities that specialise in recycling furniture. You can search for a charity in your area on the Charity Commission's website: www.charity-commission.gov.uk.

And finally… You should thank the agent for their involvement in the sale or purchase of your property. If they've carried out even a small majority of the steps in this book, they've been very busy. Fingers crossed, you reap the rewards for years to come with your fantastic new property.

In Conclusion...

If you're browsing through this book, and you are anything at all like me, you'll have flicked straight to this last chapter to see if there's anything worth taking away (some people call this cheating the author, or being lazy. I prefer to think of it as being time-efficient).

So, there are a few final points I'd like to reiterate. See it as a two-minute summary, highlighting the most important of my 101 tips...Just for you *time-efficient* readers out there...

- Be certain of your ultimate goal and remain motivated, pro-active and objective throughout the process to achieve the best possible outcome.
- Be prepared – and rely only on yourself.
- The Internet will be your best friend during this process.
- Don't get emotionally attached. It's not personal.
- Spend time deciding which agent to instruct – it can make all the difference in achieving that extra £10,000.
- It's not what you pay when you get *on* the property ladder, but what you achieve when you get off that matters.
- The secret to successful negotiation is silence. State your offer and then shh.
- You'll get more value from the process if you treat your agent, solicitor and buyer (or vendor) in a decent manner.
- Finally, you must remember, you're buying a home. Love where you live.

Useful Organisations and Trade Bodies

The Property Ombudsman
Beckett House
4 Bridge Street
Salisbury
Wiltshire SP1 2LX
☎ 01722 333306
🖥 www.oea.co.uk

Ombudsman Services: Property
PO Box 1021
Warrington WA4 9FE
☎ 01925 530 270
🖥 www.os-property.org

**National Association
of Estate Agents**
Arbon House
21 Jury Street
Warwick CV34 4EH
☎ 01926 496800
🖥 www.naea.co.uk

**Royal Institution of
Chartered Surveyors**
Surveyor Court
Westwood Way
Coventry CV4 8JE
☎ 0870 333 1600
🖥 www.rics.org.uk

The Law Society
The Law Society's Hall
113 Chancery Lane
London WC2A 1PL
☎ 020 7242 1222
🖥 www.lawsociety.org.uk

Solicitors Regulation Authority
Ipsley Court
Berrington Close
Redditch B98 0TD
☎ 0870 606 2555
🖥 www.sra.org.uk

Leaseholders Advisory Service
Maple House
149 Tottenham Court Road
London W1T 7BN
☎ 020 7383 9800
🖥 www.lease-advice.org

Land Registry
32 Lincoln's Inn Fields
London WC2A 3PH
☎ 020 7917 8888
🖥 www.landreg.gov.uk

Some Friendly Service Providers Who'll Help You on the Ladder

(and were of great assistance during the writing of this book)

Solicitors

Ingram Winter Green Solicitors
Bedford House
21A John Street
London WC1N 2BF
☎ 020 7845 7400
✉ info@iwg.co.uk
💻 www.iwg.co.uk

Downs Solicitors and Notaries
The Tanners
75 Meadrow
Godalming
Surrey GU7 3HU
☎ 01483 861848
💻 www.downslaw.co.uk

Independent Financial Advisors

Greene Financial Services
Suite A, 1/3 Canfield Place
West Hampstead
London NW6 3BT
☎ 020 7328 3280
✉ enquiries@greenefs.co.uk
💻 www.greenefs.co.uk

Surveyors

Andrew M. Lester MRICS
AML Surveys and Valuation Ltd
4 Burrows Road
London NW10 5SG
☎ 020 8960 7573
✉ andrew.m.lester@btinternet.com

Floorplans and Virtual Tours

Photoplan
Canalot Studios
222 Kensal Road
London W10 5BN
☎ 0845 094 0877
✉ orders@photoplan.co.uk
💻 www.photoplan.co.uk

House Doctor

Pad of London
☎ 0845 388 0380
💻 www.padoflondon.com

Auctioneer

Essential Information Group Ltd
The Property Auction Specialists
9 Castlefield Road
Reigate
Surrey RH2 0SA
☎ 01737 232 289
✉ davids@eigroup.co.uk

Recommended Reading

Books

Getting to Yes
Negotiating Agreement Without Giving In
Roger Fisher, William Ury and Bruce Patton (Bantam Books, 1991)

Pay off Your Mortgage in 2 Years
Your Fast Track to Financial Freedom
Graham Hooper (BBC Books, 2006)

Renovating for Profit
Add Value to Your Property with this Definitive Guide
Michael Homes, Editor-in-Chief of *Homebuilding and Renovations Magazine* (Ebury Press, 2008)

The DIY Decorator's Handbook
M.R. Light (New Holland, 2010)

Good Housekeeping 101 DIY Fixes!
Your Handy Guide to Quick Jobs, Repairs and Renovations
(Anova Books, 2010)

The Energy Efficient Home
Paul Wagland and Laura Cook
(Guild of Master Craftsman Publications, 2009)

Clear Your Clutter with Feng Shui
Karen Kingston (Piatkus, 2009)

Top Ten Investments of the Next 10 Years
Jim Mellon and Al Chalabi (Capstone Publishing, 2008)

Sarah Beeny's Green Your Home
Your Guide to Eco-friendly Renovations and Repairs
(Anova Books, 2009)

The Real Deal
My Story from Brick Lane to the Dragons' Den
James Caan (Virgin Books, 2008)

Websites

L. Michael Hall, Ph.D. (ISNS) International Society of Neuro-Semantics
www.neurosemantics.com

Mortgage calculators
www.bbc.co.uk/homes/property/mortgagecalculator.shtml
www.mortgagecalculator.org.uk

Property portals *(This is not by any means a definitive list!)*
www.rightmove.co.uk
www.zoopla.co.uk
www.globrix.com
www.findaproperty.com

www.primelocation.com
www.zoomf.co.uk
www.homesandproperty.co.uk
www.lookforaproperty.co.uk

Local area information
www.upmystreet.com

Local council details
www.direct.gov.uk

Sold data
www.landreg.gov.uk

Surveyors
www.rics.org

Finance info
www.fsa.gov.uk
www.moneymadeclear.org.uk
www.moneysupermarket.com

Structural engineers
www.istructe.org
www.localsurveyorsdirect.co.uk

Architects
www.architecture.com

Legal help
www.communitylegaladvice.org.uk
www.lawsociety.org.uk
www.adviceguide.org.uk

Removal companies
www.uk-removal.co.uk

The Balcony Form 1

Property facts for: (insert address)

....

The asking price:..

The offer:..

What does the asking price include? ....

Exchange period? ....

Completion period? ....

THE VALUE

In order to proceed in a sensible way at least one of the following has to be ticked.

Which of these is the property's value based upon?

☐ The average of three agents' valuations.

☐ The buyable price of three similar properties.

☐ Information from three local agents concerning other similar properties which have been sold.

☐ Your own research via the Land Registry of three similar properties which have been sold.

☐ The opinion of a local independent surveyor or valuer.

The Balcony Form 2

VENDOR'S POSITION. THE FACTS.

How long has the property been on the market? ....

What time scale period are the vendors working to? ....

Have there been any abortive sales and why? ....

....

....

Can I establish how many buyers have been to view the property?

....

Can I establish how many genuine offers have there been?

....

What price might the vendor accept now? ....

What price will they accept in one month's time? ....

What price in two months' time? ....

As an independent person and knowing all the
above, what price should the vendor accept today? ....

Why is the vendor looking for the price they are?........................

....

Do any of their circumstances allow them to take less? ....

If the national press is correct how much
will this property be worth in six months' time? ....

The Balcony Form 3

BUYER'S POSITION. THE FACTS.

How much is the buyer looking to go up to? ....

Have they got their mortgage arranged in principle? ....

How long have they been looking? ....

How many properties have they been to see? ....

What are they basing their offer on? ....

Is their offer realistic? ....

Will they go up? And can they afford to? ....

If you were the buyer, what is the maximum
price you would pay for the property? ....

If a sale is not agreed for this property,
do you think the buyer will still be
around to purchase it in a month's time? ....

Why is the buyer offering this price? ....

Are they being sensible or not? ....

What mortgage offer do they have? ....

The Balcony Form 4

BEST ALTERNATIVE TO A NEGOTIATED AGREEMENT (BATNA)*
Vendor

If the vendor doesn't agree to
this deal what will happen? ....

Will they be able to wait for another buyer? ....

How desperate are they? ....

How much time have they got? ....

Will someone else buy the property quickly? ....

If you were the vendor what would you do? ....

What are the financial implications
of not accepting the offer? ....

Do they strike you as desperate sellers? ....

Purchaser

Why is the purchaser making the offer at this price? ....

Are they right and why? ....

Will the purchaser increase their offer?......................................

What are their options? ....

If their offer isn't accepted what will happen to them next? ....

Have they signed the Goodwill Charter*?...................................

* for more information on Goodwill Charters and BATNAs, see chapters 15 and 50.

The Goodwill Charter

THIS AGREEMENT is made on the ____day of _____ , 20____

BETWEEN

1.   [_____] (1) ("the Seller") and

2.   [_____] (2) ("the Buyer")

3.   [_____] ("the Agent") of

      [_____] (3) ("Address")

THE parties agree as follows:

1. DEFINITIONS AND INTERPRETATIONS

In this agreement, unless the context otherwise requires:

1.1   "**Lockout Period**" means the period from and including today's date and expiring at 5.30pm on the first working day following the date which is [_____] (4) days after the date upon which the Buyer's Solicitors receive a Complete Package (as defined) from the Seller's Solicitors

1.2   "**a Complete Package**" means

1.2.1 In the case of a leasehold property such of the following documents as may be appropriate in all the circumstances:

    A   A draft Contract

    B   Office Copy entries of the Seller's Title and office Copy filed plan

    C   A copy of the Seller's Lease

    D   Evidence of the Landlord's and Superior Landlord's requirements for consent to the sale to be given

    E   An up to date buildings insurance schedule

    F   Copies of the last three years service charge accounts

    G   An up to date buildings insurance schedule

    H   Replies to standard preliminary enquiries before contract on such forms as may be deemed appropriate by the Seller's Solicitors

    I   A completed fixtures and fittings form

      J   Any other documents reasonably necessary for the Buyer's Solicitors to certify good and marketable title to the Buyer's Lenders

1.2.2 In the case of Freehold property such of the following documents as may be appropriate in all the circumstances:

      A   A draft Contract

      B   Office Copy entries of the Seller's Title and Office Copy filed plan

      C   Replies to standard preliminary enquiries before contract on such forms as may be deemed appropriate by the Seller's Solicitors

      D   A completed fixtures and fittings form

      E   Any other documents reasonably necessary for the Buyer's Solicitors to certify good and marketable title to the Buyer's Lenders

1.3   **"the Property"** means the property known as [_____] (5) described in the Agents' particulars a copy of which is attached

1.4   **"Bond"** means the sum of £ [_____] (6) which is to be paid by both parties to the Agents in cleared funds on or before today's date. For the avoidance of doubt this means that the Seller will pay a bond of £ [_____] (6) and the Buyer will also pay a bond of £ [_____] (6).

1.5   **"Solicitors"** includes licensed conveyancers or anyone acting in a legal capacity or representing either party in the conveyancing process

2   SELLER'S PROMISE

In consideration of the Bond paid by the Buyer to the Agent (receipt of which the Agent acknowledges) and in consideration of the Buyer's promises set out in this agreement the Seller undertakes with the Buyer as follows:

2.1   To procure that the Seller's Solicitors send within seven days of today a Complete Package for the sale of the Property to the Buyer's Solicitors and not to instruct them to withdraw the draft Contract (nor any of the papers contained in the Complete Package within the Lockout Period

2.2   Not during the Lockout Period:

2.2.1 To market the Property to anyone other than the Buyer; or

2.2.2 To invite, entertain or accept subject to contract an offer for the purchase of or any other dealing with the Seller's interest in the Property from any third party; or

2.2.3 To sell or enter into an agreement to sell or otherwise dispose of the Seller's interest in the Property to any third party; or

2.2.4   To instruct the Seller's Solicitors to submit a draft contract nor any other papers whatsoever for the proposed sale of the Property to solicitors acting for any other party; or

2.2.5   Otherwise to negotiate with any third party for the sale of the Property to that or any other third party.

2.3   To co-operate fully with the Seller's Solicitors in dealing with any matters raised by the Buyer's solicitors on the documents supplied to them with a view to affording to the Buyer every reasonable opportunity to the ready to enter into an unconditional binding agreement with the Seller for the purchase of the Property within the Lockout Period.

3   BUYER'S PROMISE

In consideration of the Bond paid by the Seller to the Agent (receipt of which the Agent acknowledges) and in consideration of the Seller's promises set out in this agreement the Buyer undertakes with the Seller as follows to take all reasonable steps to progress its pre-contract searches enquiries and investigation of title and any necessary financial arrangements (including any valuation report or structural survey report as the buyer may require) with a view to being ready to enter into a binding agreement with the Seller for the purchase of the Property within the Lockout Period.

4   THE AGENT'S PROMISE

4.1   The Agent agrees with both parties that it will hold the Bond in accordance with the terms of this Agreement and should the Bond be payable by one party to the other as a result of that party's default then the Agent will forthwith pay the Bond to the party who is not in default (together with that party's own Bond).

4.2   In the event that contracts are exchanged for the sale and purchase of the Property the Bond paid by both parties under the terms of this Agreement shall be repaid by the Agent to both parties.

4.3   The Agent shall act reasonably and fairly at all times and shall have the discretion to pay the Bond to a party who is not in default of the terms of this Agreement if it considers that the other party is in default and the Agent's decision shall be final and binding on the parties hereto.

5 AGREEMENT

5.1 The parties will act towards each other at all times in good faith with honesty and integrity and shall use all reasonable endeavours to ensure the observance of the terms of this Agreement.

5.2 If the Buyer's solicitors do not within the Lockout Period lodge with the Seller's Solicitors a signed contract and 10% deposit (by solicitors client account cheque, building society cheque, bankers draft or telegraphic transfer) (or such other deposit as may be agreed between the parties within the Lockout Period) for the unconditional purchase of the Property at the price of

£ [＿＿＿＿＿] (7) (or such other price as may be agreed between the parties) within the Lockout Period then the Buyer shall forfeit the Bond and the Seller shall retain it absolutely.

5.3 If, after the Buyer has so lodged a signed contract and deposit in accordance with the previous paragraph, the Seller does not within three days thereof (whether or not within the Lockout Period) exchange contracts with the Buyer then the Seller shall forfeit the Bond which shall belong to the Buyer absolutely.

6 ARBITRATION

In the event of dispute between the parties as to any provision of this Agreement such dispute shall be referred on the application of either party to an arbitrator appointed by the President of the time being of the Royal Institution of Chartered Surveyors on the application of either party and the decision of such arbitrator shall be final and binding on the parties hereto and his costs payable as he shall determine.

Signed by the Seller ....

Signed by the Buyer ....

Signed by the Agent ....

SELLING GANTT CHART

	MONTH 1				MONTH 2				M
	Wk 1	Wk 2	Wk 3	Wk 4	Wk 5	Wk 6	Wk 7	Wk 8	W
Consider / decide if selling is your best option	▓								
Research local property prices online	▓	▓							
Mystery shop estate agents (and check they're registered with compulsory schemes)		▓	▓						
Instruct solicitor and have deeds and searches made available			▓	▓	▓	▓	▓	▓	▓
Prepare a draft contract			▓	▓					
Invite Surveyor for informal valuation and any major defects				▓					
Invite 3-5 agents to your home for a valuation					▓				
Decide on price you want to market and instruct agent(s)						▓	▓		
Instruct DEA to conduct EPC							▓		
Sit down with agent to discuss marketing and sales plan							▓		
Have property clean and tidy for photographs/viewings							▓	▓	▓
Consider employing services of house doctor to clear clutter/make most of your home							▓		
Prepare home and security for viewings							▓	▓	▓
Receive offer									
Understand your buyer, their position and complete balcony form. Determine B.A.T.N.A.									
Accept offer and propose Goodwill Charter									
Exchange									
Complete									

9	Wk 10	Wk 11	Wk 12	Wk 13	Wk 14	Wk 15	Wk 16	Wk 17	Wk 18	Wk 19
▓	▓	▓	▓	▓	▓	▓	▓	▓	▓	▓
▓	▓									
▓	▓									
	▓									
▓	▓	▓								
		▓								
						▓				
										▓